Cambridge Elements

Elements in the Philosophy of Martin Heidegger
edited by
Filippo Casati
Lehigh University
Daniel O. Dahlstrom
Boston University

HEIDEGGER ON THINKING

Lee Braver
University of South Florida

Shaftesbury Road, Cambridge CB2 8EA, United Kingdom

One Liberty Plaza, 20th Floor, New York, NY 10006, USA

477 Williamstown Road, Port Melbourne, VIC 3207, Australia

314–321, 3rd Floor, Plot 3, Splendor Forum, Jasola District Centre, New Delhi – 110025, India

103 Penang Road, #05–06/07, Visioncrest Commercial, Singapore 238467

Cambridge University Press is part of Cambridge University Press & Assessment, a department of the University of Cambridge.

We share the University's mission to contribute to society through the pursuit of education, learning and research at the highest international levels of excellence.

www.cambridge.org
Information on this title: www.cambridge.org/9781009466950
DOI: 10.1017/9781009466929

© Lee Braver 2024

This publication is in copyright. Subject to statutory exception and to the provisions of relevant collective licensing agreements, no reproduction of any part may take place without the written permission of Cambridge University Press & Assessment.

When citing this work, please include a reference to the DOI 10.1017/9781009466929

First published 2024

A catalogue record for this publication is available from the British Library.

ISBN 978-1-009-46695-0 Hardback
ISBN 978-1-009-46694-3 Paperback
ISSN 2976-5668 (online)
ISSN 2976-565X (print)

Cambridge University Press & Assessment has no responsibility for the persistence or accuracy of URLs for external or third-party internet websites referred to in this publication and does not guarantee that any content on such websites is, or will remain, accurate or appropriate.

Heidegger on Thinking

Elements in the Philosophy of Martin Heidegger

DOI: 10.1017/9781009466929
First published online: October 2024

Lee Braver
University of South Florida
Author for correspondence: Lee Braver, lbraver@usf.edu

Abstract: Every philosophy is a celebration of the fact that being can be thought, that the world around us yields to concepts that join together into arguments which can lead us to new thoughts and new ways of thinking. Heidegger's great talent was to never lose his philosophical wonder at philosophy, to never stop thinking about thinking. Heidegger's early work favors a somewhat pragmatic view of thinking as organized by and around our projects, emphasizing tacit skills over articulate conscious thinking. It also explores stepping back from all projects in dread and wonder. His later thinking is reciprocal rather than autonomous, something we do with and for being instead of something we do to or on beings, which can help overcome contemporary nihilism. After the death of God, we may no longer be able to pray to a divinity, but we can still be the thinkers of being.

Keywords: Heidegger, thinking, thought, concepts, intelligence

© Lee Braver 2024

ISBNs: 9781009466950 (HB), 9781009466943 (PB), 9781009466929 (OC)
ISSNs: 2976-5668 (online), 2976-565X (print)

Contents

Introduction: What Is Called Thinking by Heidegger?   1

Part I Early Heidegger   3

Part II Later Heidegger: Thoughtful Thinking   23

Conclusion: Thinking in Question   48

Bibliography   57

Introduction: What Is Called Thinking by Heidegger?

> Much rests on knowing what this means: thinking.
> Heidegger, *Bremen and Freiburg Lectures Insight into That Which Is and Basic Principles of Thinking*

> We come to know what it means to think when we ourselves try to think. If the attempt is to be successful, we must be ready to learn thinking.
> Heidegger, *What Is Called Thinking?*

Despite the fact that Descartes said it,[1] it still is true that we are essentially thinkers – we just have to define what that means. Heidegger would agree with the statement and argue that thinking it at a deep level requires us to rethink every word in it: we, are, essentially, thinkers.

We think: thinking is not something I do on my own, sitting alone in a cabin with the world placed at a distance. We think with and within a historically situated community, one that makes us who we are as we reciprocally let it be what it is. I can never think except from a we and with a we; no *one* can.

We are. It's not that we are because we think but that we think because we are as thinkers. One reason the question of being necessarily comes is that all things do what they do because they are what they are, although this very point starts breaking down these distinctions. For Heidegger, all inquiries must look to the kind of being of the entity being inquired into.

We are essentially. Essences for Heidegger are more like active engagements than properties or states; he sometimes uses an older form of the word for essence as a verb: *wesen*, 'to essence.' To be is to behave in certain ways through time rather than sitting stolidly self-identically.

We essence as thinkers. One of the main ways that we are is by thinking, getting struck by ideas, wondering and dwelling on them, seeking explanations and gathering reasons to make sense of our lives. Thoughts are not preliminaries to action but are our highest activity, our *ergon* to use Aristotle's term. Thus, to know ourselves, we must think about thinking. Most philosophers do, but few give it the deep, sustained pondering that Heidegger did. Heidegger dwelt on thinking; he made it his philosophical dwelling.

The project of *Being and Time*, his early magnum opus, is to understand being. However, to understand the deepest, broadest, most perplexing, and, at the same time, closest and simplest topic there is, we have to understand how we understand anything at all. We must first understand understanding in order to understand what it is to understand being. You could say, then, that the entire book is ultimately about thinking.

---

[1] "I am, then, in the strict sense only a thing that thinks" (Descartes/ed. Cottingham et al., 2013, 18).

The part of the book that got published[2] is a sustained attempt to understand us insofar as we can be aware of anything – what he calls "Dasein." This "existential analytic" is intended to serve as the foundation of the study of being, which may strike some as something of a non sequitur (Heidegger, 1962, 34/13). It's justified when we think about the interdependence between the meaning of being and a being that can understand it. Think about seeing. We discover the visibility of being by studying human sight, which we get at by examining the anatomy of the eyeball, the visual part of the brain, and so on. Understanding how we see tells us what we can see, and so what of reality can be seen. Similarly, we analyze Dasein's way of being in order to fully comprehend our understanding, which will show us what it means for anything to be understandable – the meaning of being (Heidegger, 1962, 424/372). This is the basic strategy of *Being and Time*.

Division I of the book favors something of a pragmatic view of thinking, according to which it is organized by and around our projects. This innovative conception emphasizes tacit skills over articulate conscious thinking, know-how more than knowing-that. Division II then turns to a more existential stepping back from all projects in a mood of existential dread that liberates us to become authentic.

Wonder, the beginning of philosophy for Plato and Aristotle, comes to the forefront in his later thoughts. As perhaps the only thinkers in existence, we have a kind of responsibility to respond thoughtfully to being's provocations and solicitations to think. This should not be carried out as a grave duty but rather celebrated as a festival.

Heidegger's later work portrays thinking as reciprocal instead of the traditional view of spontaneous, autonomous control, the source of transcendental philosophy, technology, and nihilism. Thinking becomes something we do with and for being instead of to beings on our own for ourselves. It is a cooperation rather than a cooptation, a releasement of thoughts rather than a grasping of concepts, an attending and tending to beings that allows them to come forth and fully be what they are, like nurturing a plant to its flourishing. This account of reason may help overcome the nihilism that he thinks traditional notions of thinking have led us into. After the death of God we may no longer be able to be worshipful servants of a divinity, but we can still be the thinkers of being, standing in awe before the fact that anything is at all.

Every painting tells us to cherish and delight in the way the world fits our vision, beauty raising the two into their reciprocal essencing height. Every piece

---

[2] See Braver, 2015b for a number of Heidegger experts' views on what the missing portion might have been like.

of music is a revelling in hearing. So philosophizing is a celebration of the fact that being can be thought, that the world around us yields to concepts that join together into arguments which can lead us to entirely new ways of thinking which in turn open up further ways of celebrating the world and living out our lives. Along with everything else that it is, an argument is a work of art in the medium of ideas, and all works of art carry the same message: "at bottom, the ordinary is not ordinary; it is extraordinary" (Heidegger, 1993a, 179). The simplest, most ubiquitous fact there is – the fact *of* the there is – is what there now is for us, and it is astonishing in its unsurpassable mundanity. "Everything in what is most usual (beings) becomes in wonder the most unusual in this one respect: that it is what it is" (Heidegger, 1994a, 144). There are, of course, many themes in the decades of his later thought, but they all gather around our thinking of being in some way or other. Heidegger's great talent was to never stop being amazed, to never lose his philosophical wonder or stop thinking about thinking, everything he writes being an invitation to join him at the "feast of thought" (Heidegger, 1993a, 144).

There are two parts to this Element, dividing along the main turn in Heidegger's own path of thinking. Part I examines Heidegger's early thinking and view of thinking as it surfaces in Divisions I and II of *Being and Time*. Part II turns to the way of thinking Heidegger took in later years. The aim throughout is to unpack both how he thinks and what he takes thinking to be, i.e., what he shows us and what he says about thinking. I will be organizing the Parts around short statements about what thinking is for Heidegger – e.g., "thinking is interested," "thinking is temporal," "thinking is wondrous," and so on – each of which will serve as something like a thesis statement for its section.

Part I Early Heidegger

> We can learn thinking only if we radically unlearn what thinking has been traditionally.
> Heidegger, *What Is Called Thinking?*, 8

I Division I of *Being and Time*: Thoughtful Knowing-How to Get Around in the World

Thinking Thinks the History of Thinking

From the beginning to the end of his long career, Heidegger believed that thinking is historical. Thinking takes place as a conversation *with* the tradition because it takes place *within* the tradition, as our predecessors give place to us. "Our own way derives from such [traditional] thinking. It therefore remains necessarily bound to a dialogue with traditional thinking. And since our way is concerned with thinking for the specific purpose of learning it, the dialogue must discuss the nature of traditional thinking" (Heidegger, 1968, 55). Thinking about thinking is, of course, itself an act of thinking, being both the topic thought about and the thinking about it. This makes all these thoughts we'll be looking at reflexive because any conclusions they reach about their subject automatically apply to themselves. If thinking is historical, then, thinking of the historicality of thought must be as well: thinking about historical thinking can only be done historically. Most thinkers do so naively, unaware of the context informing their inquiry or even in denial of it. Understanding the nature of thinking, however, requires us to fully appreciate how that context informs all inquiry, including that one.

Thinking of thinking must, dizzyingly, become a historical thinking of the history of thinking about historical thinking, as Heidegger realizes in the Introduction to *Being and Time*:

> The ownmost meaning of Being which belongs to the inquiry into Being as an historical inquiry, gives us the assignment of inquiring into the history of that inquiry itself . . . . By positively making the past our own, we may bring ourselves into full possession of the ownmost possibilities of such inquiry. The question of the meaning of Being . . . thus brings itself to the point where it understands itself as historiological. (Heidegger, 1962, 42/20–21)

To move forward, inquiry must go back. To think about thinking in a new way requires a thoughtful immersion in the old ways, and much of Heidegger's work is taken up with examinations of previous philosophers' thoughts about the nature of thought.

Traditional Thinking Thinks of Thinking as Articulate and Thematic

When Socrates questioned people in his dialogues, he demanded that they come up with explicit, articulate definitions that captured the essence of their subject in logically consistent accounts. The interlocutors' inability to do so exposed their lack of knowledge and, perhaps more importantly, their lack of thinking. The fact that they did not realize how shabby their beliefs were showed how little examination they had given them. Since beliefs determine actions for Socrates, living the unexamined life meant believing unexamined beliefs, whereas the life worth living is dedicated to thinking through one's thoughts, poring over them and improving them until they can withstand Socrates' examination. Only explicit, thematic analysis can determine the worth of thoughts and yield truth; its absence can give, at best, lucky guesses. This has been one of the models, if not the primary model of thinking and knowledge in philosophy ever since. Let us call it the Platonic Model.[3]

---

[3] Of course, there are multiple interpretations of Plato, many of which would diverge from this reading.

We can see the Platonic Model in, for example, Augustine's famous frustration about time: when no one asks him what time is, he can deal with it perfectly well; but if anyone asks him to define it, he suddenly has no idea what to say, paralyzed like Socrates' interlocutors. His theoretical inability to tell us what time is undermines for him his practical ability to tell what time it is.[4] To generalize extravagantly, most philosophers have followed Plato's lead, leaving another epistemological path relatively unexplored: what would happen if we take seriously that mundane capability to deal with time, the know-how of timing and showing up on time that Augustine scoffs at? Perhaps wandering down such paths heretofore relatively untraveled is one way, "by positively making the past our own, we may bring ourselves into full possession of the ownmost possibilities of such inquiry" (Heidegger, 1962, 42/21).

Heidegger wrote on Aristotle a great deal and he took a few steps down this path. Plato says that knowledge is virtue – you must know what virtue is in order to be virtuous and just knowing it makes you virtuous. But for Aristotle, virtue is knowledge – if you behave virtuously and demonstrate virtue in your actions, then you ipso facto possess the relevant knowledge. "Some people who lack knowledge but have experience are better in action than others who have knowledge" (Aristotle, 2019, VI.7.1141b16-19). The skill is not a rudimentary approximation or preparatory step to its true form of a logical, articulated account. No, this kind of thinking and knowledge is embodied in its enactment.

<u>Thinking Is Pragmatic</u>. Most philosophers base their views of human nature on some specialized, atypical quality or activity – usually theoretical contemplation, though others such as worship or citizenship crop up here and there. Instead of understanding us beginning from what we do one percent of the time, Heidegger wants to start from what we do ninety-nine percent of the time – our average everydayness where our thinking is wrapped up in what we are doing rather than a matter of abstract rumination. "I cannot adequately define the concept of understanding if, in trying to make the definition, I look solely to specific types of cognitive comportment" (Heidegger, 1988, 275).

So what do we do most of the time? Well, we *do* stuff – we drive cars, eat sandwiches, go swimming, as well as several other things. We act, interacting with things and people to accomplish goals, and we do this far more and much earlier than abstract thinking.[5] Many argue that all of that behavior can only take

---

[4] Note: while I have been using a theory–practice dichotomy to get the basic ideas across quickly and easily, Heidegger's more complete account rejects any such clean division. Contemplation, after all, is one of the duties of a professional philosopher, as I inform my wife when she tells me that I'm not paid to think.

[5] Some scholars, such as Richard Rorty (1979, 1982, 1991) and Mark Okrent (1988), have found common ground between Heidegger's views and American pragmatism, as did Dewey. "Sidney Hook reports, for instance, that John Dewey, after hearing a summary of *Being and Time*,

place on the basis of intellectual convictions. I picked up the hammer because I held the belief that hammering in nails is the best way to build this bookshelf, that building this bookshelf is a good thing to do, and that this is a hammer. Thinking must always be present before and beneath our actions, rather than just generally going along thoughtlessly.

Heidegger argues that most of the time when we hammer, we're just hammering. There need not be any explicit thoughts about the hammer or the goal or really anything at all. We retroactively place beliefs underneath our actions when we stop acting to theoretically reconstruct what had been happening, bullied into a belief in beliefs by the tradition's cognitivism. "I picked up the hammer, so I must have had the thought that that's what it was." This is not a good phenomenological description of what actually occurred but rather an artifact of the tradition's influence (as well as another reason we will soon discuss). If we describe what actually happened more carefully, we come up with a very different account:

> In such dealings an entity of this kind is not grasped thematically as an occurring Thing, nor is the equipment-structure known as such even in the using. The hammering does not simply have knowledge about the hammer's character as equipment, but it has appropriated this equipment in a way which could not possibly be more suitable .... When we deal with them by using them and manipulating them, this activity is not a blind one; it has its own kind of sight, by which our manipulation is guided. (Heidegger, 1962, 98/69)

The notion that there *had* to be some cognitive element like knowledge or belief motivating or justifying our action is not supported by the evidence but by a twenty-five-century-long presupposition.

The point isn't that we use things *instead* of understanding them. That takes the Platonic Model as the only genuine form of knowledge so that if we lack that, we simply have nothing. Of course I understood the tool – I picked up the lump of metal with a stick of wood attached and slammed a piece of metal into some boards with it; I didn't use it to pick up a cat or eat soup. Picking out the right item and using it appropriately gives clear evidence of understanding, but one that doesn't fit the Platonic Model of understanding well. Heidegger argues that a distinct form of understanding is operative in our activities that, if captured in cognitive terms, can only appear as a poor form of contemplation, as it did to Augustine who scorned his ability to meet his friends for lunch at noon. This is understanding not in the sense of having thematic knowledge but "with the signification of 'being able to manage something'" (Heidegger, 1962, 183/143);

---

remarked 'that it sounded as if a German peasant were trying to render parts of [Dewey's book] *Experience and Nature* into his daily idiom'" (Guignon, 1983, 1).

one understands "in the sense of being skilled or expert at it, has the know-how of it" (Heidegger, 1988, 276). This know-how is clearly a kind of intelligence but one which operates with completely different rules from the Platonic Model's knowing-that:

> We are after the most common kind of everyday perception and not a perception in the emphatic sense, in which we observe only for the sake of observing. Natural perception as I live in it in moving about my world is for the most part not a detached observation and scrutiny of things, but is rather absorbed in dealing with the matters at hand concretely and practically ... to pave the way in dealing with something. (Heidegger, 1985, 30)

He calls this intelligence "circumspection" [*Umsicht*] (Heidegger, 1962, 98/69) and a good bit of Division I is spent delineating its features along with the things it understands (equipment) and the being who understands them (Dasein).[6]

This has proven to be a fruitful and influential idea. It formed an important inspiration for the work of Hubert Dreyfus, arguably the most important American Heidegger scholar.[7] In the mid-1960s, the RAND corporation asked him to evaluate early AI work.[8] In order to make an *artificial* intelligence, he realized, one had to have a good sense of what intelligence is. Drawing on Heidegger, along with Meleau-Ponty and Wittgenstein, Dreyfus concluded that the programmers' work was unlikely to succeed because it used the Platonic Model of thinking, which came to be called GOFAI for Good Old-Fashioned AI.[9] The GOFAI model tried to construct thinkers out of enormous sets of facts and rules; these were the kinds of things a computer could compute and they fit Socrates' demands. But, as Heidegger argued, "understanding can never be gained by amassing a large quantity of information and proofs. On the contrary, all knowing, cognitive proving, and the producing of arguments, sources, and the like always already presuppose understanding" (Heidegger, 1985, 259–260). The most powerful computers' inability to comprehend what a four-year-old can grasp with ease served as a *reductio* of GOFAI's conception of intelligence. There has sprung up in his wake a minor school of Heideggerian programming and Rodney Brooks, the later head of robotics at Massachusetts Institute of

---

[6] Two excellent books on the contrast between *Being and Time* and traditional epistemology are Charles Guignon's *Heidegger and the Problem of Knowledge* and John Richardson's *Existential Epistemology: A Heideggerian Critique of the Cartesian Project*.

[7] Dreyfus also allegedly served as the model for Professor Hubert J. Farnsworth in the TV show *Futurama*. The only academic achievement I ever had that impressed my kids was having Professor Farnsworth blurb my book.

[8] Dreyfus describes this in *What Computers Still Can't Do*, *Mind Over Machine*, and "Overcoming the Myth of the Mental." See *Mind, Reason, and Being-in-the-World: The McDowell-Dreyfus Debate* for an extensive discussion of this topic.

[9] See Haugeland, 1985; Winograd and Flores, 1986; Clark, 1998; Kiverstein and Wheeler, 2012.

Technology, has said that he finds (what he has heard of) Heidegger's thought to be close to his own work (Brooks, 1991).

Dreyfus and his brother also combined Heidegger's ideas with empirical research to devise a multiple-stage model of skill acquisition. This places conscious thought at the beginning and the bottom: when we are first learning a skill, we have to self-consciously and rigidly obey rules with crude and clumsy results. As our aptitude increases, conscious control and even awareness fade out until we can achieve the state that psychologist Csikszentmihalyi calls "flow." This is the complete absorption in what we're doing that produces the most skilled activity. Athletes who start consciously thinking about their actions drop down levels until their explicit awareness submerges once more, overturning the traditional privilege that conscious thematic thinking has enjoyed over tacit action. While philosophers have generally cited people's lack of thinking as a profound flaw – leading to lives not worth living – Heidegger argues that this nonthematic engagement is a distinct and legitimate form of mental activity, one that is superior to contemplation in the vast majority of situations we find ourselves in.

Thinking Is Interested. Heidegger thus sets aside the traditional image of cold, objective logic as the core of thought for circumspection. This is motivated by what he calls care, the next level down in his existential analytic of Dasein which lies beneath and accounts for our being-in-the-world. You are in-the-world by pursuing your projects and you do what you do because it matters to you who you are. This view of thinking as intrinsically interested diverges widely from the traditional disinterested subject contemplating the world as a separate object.

Circumspection is primarily directed at equipment (what Heidegger calls ready-to-hand beings), but that is a very broad category. It can encompass not just hammers and baseball gloves but just about anything you use or interact with in the course of going about your daily affairs. Circumspection is engaged and motivated; you only seek out equipment in pursuit of a desired goal and can only recognize something *as* a tool by seeing how it gets you want you want. You pick up the hammer not to learn the objective truth about it but because you want to build a bookshelf, which in turn you want in order to put your books on, so that you can be the professional scholar you want to be. This is the know-how we live in everyday. "The kind of dealing which is closest to us is as we have shown, not a bare perceptual cognition, but rather that kind of concern which manipulates things and puts them to use; and this has its own kind of 'knowledge'" (Heidegger, 1962, 95/67). This is a kind of thinking because it deals intelligently with the world, orienting our understanding of it and action in it, all in terms of a meaning – just one that is generally not articulated or thematic.

Heidegger on Thinking 9

> The kind of being belonging to letting the world be encountered in the primary mode of concern is itself one of *understanding* .... This primary state of knowing one's way about belongs essentially to in-being .... But this implies that understanding primarily does not mean a mode of knowing at all, unless knowing itself has been seen as a constitutive state of being for being-in-the-world .... Understanding absorption in the world *discovers* the world, the referential connections in what they uniquely are, in their *meaning*. An understanding concern thus encounters what is understood – *meaning*. (Heidegger, 1985, 209)

Since it is the understanding of the meaning of being that the book is after, this reformation and expansion of what that means is an important step.

This emphasis on interestedness further distinguishes his account from the traditional one that condemns any kind of emotion or interest as biasing and distorting. Kant went so far as to say that "the inclinations themselves, being sources of needs, are so far from having an absolute value such as to render them desirable for their own sake that the universal wish of every rational being must be, rather, to be wholly free from them" (Kant, 2010, 35/428). Heidegger, however, sees moods as inextricably intermixed with thoughts – "man is not a rational creature who ... in addition to thinking and willing is equipped with feelings; ... rather, the state of feeling is original, although in such a way that thinking and willing belong together with it" (Heidegger, 1979 vol. 1, 51). Rather than being impediments to proper understanding, they are capable of revealing features of the world that cognition cannot (Heidegger, 1962, 173/134). For example, a tool can only show up as inadequate or broken to a being attempting to use it for a purpose; a hammer that's broken is still a perfectly fine piece of wood and metal:

> When something cannot be used – when, for instance, a tool definitely refuses to work – it can be conspicuous only in and for dealings in which something is manipulated. Even by the sharpest and most persevering 'perception' and 'representation' of Things, one can never discover anything like the damaging of a tool. If we are to encounter anything unmanageable, the handling must be of such a sort that it can be disturbed.[10]

Equipment can only be encountered as equipment by using it, which only occurs when one is emotionally attuned to a goal by being motivated toward it, which is

---

[10] Heidegger, 1962, 406/354–355. "To be affected by the unserviceable, resistant, or threatening character [*Bedrohlichkeit*] of that which is ready-to-hand, becomes ontologically possible only in so far as Being-in as such has been determined existentially beforehand in such a manner that what it encounters within-the-world can "*matter*" *to* it in this way. The fact that this sort of thing can 'matter' to it is grounded in one's state-of-mind .... Only something which is in the state-of-mind of fearing (or fearlessness) can discover that what is environmentally ready-to-hand is threatening. Dasein's openness to the world is constituted existentially by the attunement of a state-of-mind" (Heidegger, 1962, 176/137). See Braver 2013b.

why John Haugeland memorably said, "the trouble with artificial intelligence is that computers don't give a damn."[11]

The theoretical standpoint that has dominated philosophy originates in the change-over from ready-to-hand tools to present-at-hand objects. While working, I was lost in "a non-thematic circumspective absorption" (Heidegger, 1962, 107/76) in my world and projects. But when a tool breaks, it puts me at a distance from what I had been using, turning the inconspicuous ready-to-hand tool into a conspicuous present-at-hand object. While I'm driving along the road I don't think about the steering wheel and pedals as physical objects; I just think about what I'm going to do when I arrive, or about nothing much at all. But if the engine sputters and stops, the car suddenly pops back into focus, squeezing out everything else. It becomes present-at-hand, the kind of being that things have when we just stare at them; since philosophy inherently takes a disengaged contemplative stance, it only encounters present-at-hand objects. Metaphysicians then define the world as inert things just lying around with physical properties because that's how they show up to disinterested reflection.[12] Philosophy has always missed this kind of being because looking at the world through a contemplative eye blinds us to it. "Equipment can genuinely show itself only in dealings cut to its own measure (hammering with a hammer, for example)" (Heidegger, 1962, 98/69).

We now find ourselves needing to make a connection between our isolated thinking subject and the objects to be thought about, because our artificial stance has removed the connection that is always already there. And the only resource we have to make this connection is the one activity that is still there and so apparently defines us: thinking. Recall that Descartes found himself to be essentially a thinking thing *after* he had carefully suspended all other activities. "Today I have expressly rid my mind of all worries and arranged for myself a clear stretch of free time. I am quite alone, and at last I will devote myself sincerely and without reservation to the general demolition of my opinions" (Descartes/ed. Cottingham et al., 2013, 12). These seemingly innocuous preparations predetermined the results he could find. Our initial contact with the world seems like it can only be made by our knowing it, which raises the question of how we can be certain of this epistemological bridge from the privacy of our minds to the public world and the need to secure this certainty. Thus skepticism and foundationalism are contained in embryo in the initiating act of sitting down to just think.

---

[11] Haugeland, 1998, 47. Antonio Damasio (2015) has written extensively on the role emotion plays in cognition in *Descartes' Error: Emotion, Reason, and the Human Brain*.

[12] As with many topics in this short Element on a large topic, there is considerably more complexity that can be explored on this topic.

Thinking Is Ontological and Interpretive. Invoking ontology and interpretation may sound like a departure from my initial characterization of thinking as pragmatic and mundane, but that's only according to the view of ontology as a practice of coming up with theories. The very first page of *Being and Time* disputes this characterization when it announces, "our aim in the following treatise is to work out the question of the meaning of *Being* and to do so concretely" (Heidegger, 1962, 19/1). An inquiry into the meaning of being that can be done *concretely* must be quite different from the abstract ruminations we get from Plato or Descartes.

Heidegger firmly rejects the idea of an immediate, "presuppositionless apprehending of something presented to us" (Heidegger, 1962, 191–192/150). We interpret everything we experience, usually not in an explicit or conscious process but nevertheless one that shapes all of our experience. The "objective" characterization of the world offered by philosophy or science is simply another interpretation that is based on a particular understanding of being. It doesn't give us The World as it is independent of all Dasein but the way the world looks to us when we look at it in a particular way. "Only 'in the light' of a Nature which has been projected in this fashion can anything like a 'fact' be found.... In principle there are no 'bare facts'" (Heidegger, 1962, 414/362). Rather than being basic or foundational, he considers it derivative of our everyday pragmatic interaction. "When we merely stare at something, our just-having-it-before-us lies before us *as a failure to understand it any more*. This grasping which is free of the 'as', is a privation of the kind of seeing in which one *merely* understands. It is not more primordial than that kind of seeing, but is derived from it" (Heidegger, 1962, 190/149).

One thing that the inescapability of interpretation means is that our encounters with and uses of beings are always mediated by an understanding of their being. That does not sound like the kind of thing the average person in the street has and indeed, Heidegger does not think we have the kind of thematic articulate theory that would satisfy Socrates. We have what he calls a preontological understanding:

> One can determine the nature of entities in their Being without necessarily having the explicit concept of the meaning of Being at one's disposal .... This 'presupposing' of Being has rather the character of taking a look at it beforehand, so that in the light of it the entities presented to us get provisionally Articulated in their Being. (Heidegger, 1962, 27/7–8)

Heidegger argues that we must have a *"vague average understanding of Being"* because "we always conduct our activities in an understanding of Being" (Heidegger, 1962, 25/5). Hammers are a kind of equipment, like alarm clocks and forks, which all share a common way of being despite their differences. I must have some kind of grasp of that way of being because I know how to interact with tools in general as opposed to other types of beings. "In our dealings with what is ready-to-hand, this readiness-to-hand is itself understood, though not thematically" (Heidegger, 1962, 104/74). The fact that I know what kind of things they are and how one should generally treat them is shown by the fact that I don't ask a hammer's permission before using it whereas I would ask your permission before using you. I reflexively treat people differently than shoes (on good days) because I unconsciously ("pre-ontologically") understand their distinct types of being.

In the same way, it is only in light of our understanding of our own existence that we know that we have to act at all instead of just sitting there like a stone. Heidegger's notion of authenticity in Division II means living in a way that is appropriate to the kind beings that we are. One of the central aims of *Being and Time* (as we have it) is to correct our tendency to understand ourselves in terms of a different, inappropriate mode of being.[13] To become what we are is to grasp the nature of our existence and deliberately live in ways that are harmonious with it. Since the tradition has only supplied us with a detailed analysis and terminology suitable to presence-at-hand, Heidegger is rectifying this by giving us an existential analytic along with one of readiness-to-hand, that is, an explanation of the understanding of the being of Dasein and equipment. However, this only makes explicit what was already implicit in our behavior. As with Platonic recollection, Heidegger is not introducing something wholly new to us but rather reminding us of what we don't know that we know.

Thinking Is Social. Like many other philosophers, Kant defines reason as the ability to think for ourselves without external factors such as our society or upbringing influencing or emotions determining our conclusions. We can do this because reason is a priori and can thus close off all alien, empirical influences. Everything that impinges on our thinking is external to our true selves and must be suspended when we reason if it is truly to be *us* reasoning. This is autonomy, which is both a practical and theoretical goal in his system and can be found throughout the history of philosophy. Descartes doubted everything he had been taught just because he had been taught it, needing to reach his conclusions by his own efforts and Socrates chastises his interlocutors for mindlessly mumbling the common wisdom of their time.

---

[13] "Substructures of entities with another kind of Being (presence-at-hand or life) thrust themselves to the fore unnoticed, and threaten to bring confusion to the interpretation of this phenomenon" (Heidegger, 1962, 285/241). See my discussion of what I call the existential imperative in Braver 2014.

Division I of *Being and Time* describes Dasein as inherently social and, except for parts of Chapter IV, in generally neutral terms. "Dasein in itself is essentially Being-with" (Heidegger, 1962, 156/120) is Heidegger's version of Aristotle's "humans are a social/political [*politikon*] animal" (Aristotle, 1988, *Politics*, 1253a2-3), hence our thinking too is inescapably social. Our sociality is not a result of the fact that we happen to be around other people; it is built into us from the start. "Dasein is determined from the very outset by being-with others" (Heidegger, 1988, 296). We could not have gained our understanding of the being of others from empirical encounters with them since we would not have been able to recognize these entities *as* other people to generalize from without that category in place. "'Empathy' does not first constitute Being-with; only on the basis of Being-with does 'empathy' become possible" (Heidegger, 1962, 162/125).

The worlds I can be-in are determined by the roles available to me, and I get those roles from my society. I can only be a professor if there's a lot of institutional scaffolding supporting it: I need students, a school, general recognition of professorship as a thing, and so on. If these are lacking, then I simply cannot be a professor, no matter how professorial my behavior. Even performing all of the same actions would no longer add up to being a professor without that occupation being available. It is my society that determines what it is to be a professor by laying out the tasks that constitute it and their relevant tools, which add up to that world. "The 'they' itself articulates the referential context of significance" (Heidegger, 1962, 167/129). The "They" or the "one" [*das Man*] is Heidegger's term for what Kierkegaard names 'the crowd,' the anonymous groups in society that we assimilate ourselves to in our attempts to be someone. However, Heidegger complements this negative focus on the dangers of conformity with a more Hegelian account of the positive and indeed necessary role our social plays in constituting the possibilities we exist in and as. This public intelligibility is absolutely essential to having a world and so to being Dasein as being-in-the-world. Chapter IV of Division I of *Being and Time* gives both of these together in a brilliant but somewhat confusing mixture.

II Division II of *Being and Time*: Not Knowing How to Live, Not Knowing How to Die

<u>Thinking Is Existential/Ethical.</u> Division I of *Being and Time* describes how we habitually use tools to do some things in order to be some one. The tools recede into unnoticed inconspicuousness as we use them mindlessly, though not without understanding. He defends this "non-thematic circumspective absorption" (Heidegger, 1962, 107/76) that has been looked down on by the tradition which only recognizes explicit theoretical contemplation as legitimate thinking.

Rather than simply nonthinking, he shows it to be a distinct and fully respectable epistemological mode of its own.

When Division II returns to delve deeper into this topic, it has a more existentialist feel. Where Division I focuses on questions of knowledge and ontology, Division II uses these analyses to turn toward questions about how to live, moving from the meaning of hammers to the meaning of life.[14] However, it does not leave these discussions behind, but develops and deepens them. Division II extends the analysis of the tools we use to the lives we build with them. As the hammer withdraws as I build the bookshelf, my world as a whole withdraws and I construct my self without thinking much about it. Taking care of my daily business keeps me from giving careful consideration to the overall project it forms a part of, leading to lives lived absent-mindedly. The kind of autonomic flow that Division I rehabilitated now raises concerns for its tendency to facilitate "the oblivious passing of our lives" (Heidegger, 1988, 264), just the kind of sleep-walking that existentialists generally rail against.

We see this difference in the ways he describes the inconspicuousness of the self during everyday activities. He gives a factual description of how flow works: we must be focused on the task at hand rather than on ourselves in order to perform it smoothly.

> A specific kind of *forgetting* is essential for the temporality that is constitutive for letting something be involved. The Self must forget itself if, lost in the world of equipment, it is to be able 'actually' to go to work and manipulate something. (Heidegger, 1962, 405/354)

However, this phenomenon takes on ominous tones of existential cowardice in his analysis of inauthenticity.

> Dasein's absorption in the 'they' and its absorption in the 'world' of its concern, make manifest something like a fleeing of Dasein in the face of itself. (Heidegger, 1962, 229/184)

Here it is not a matter of activities naturally absorbing our attention but rather a motivated turning away from ourselves. We don't just naturally get lost in our work – we set out to lose ourselves.

---

[14] A couple of years after the publication of *Being and Time*, Heidegger anticipated and rejected interpretations that excessively focus on Division I's analysis of everyday tool-use: "there I took my departure from what lies to hand in the everyday realm, from those things that we use and pursue . . . . It never occurred to me, however, to try and claim or prove with this interpretation that the essence of man consists in the fact that he knows how to handle knives and forks or use the tram" (Heidegger et al., 1995, 177). Dreyfus' influential (and excellent) *Being-in-the-World: A Commentary on Heidegger's Being and Time*, focuses almost entirely on Division I.

Now achieving a state of flow leads to just go with the flow, doing what one does in our society without actively deciding. This represents a Kierkegaardian "inconspicuous domination by Others" (Heidegger, 1962, 164/126) where we do not lead our lives but follow what is expected, riding on the inertia of accepted behavior. We are defined as care, yet we live our lives carelessly.

Once our existence fades into inconspicuousness as we thoughtlessly drift along, we need something to wake us up to the fact that we're awake. This is an example of his extending Division I's analyses as he turns to the account given there of the way "the world announces itself." Usually, tools "are encountered as 'in themselves' in the concern which makes use of them without noticing them explicitly . . . . But *when an assignment has been disturbed* – when something is unusable for some purpose – then the assignment becomes explicit" (Heidegger, 1962, 105/74). We need something like the hammer breaking but on a larger scale so that it could light up our life-choices in general. Care is what pulls us into the world as we pursue our roles and goals so if this were to stop functioning, I could no longer be-in-the-world and the entire structure would break down – and thereby become conspicuous.

Care breaks down when we are struck by the fundamental mood of anxiety, which might be seen as something like clinical depression. This deep apathy toward everything one normally cares about ejects one from their world, leaving them staring at it as a strange, unfamiliar thing. When nothing seems worth doing, one's goals no longer pull one into the world of the tools used to attain them. One feels like they have been kicked out of the world and are now looking at it from the outside, temporarily being-out-of-the-world. Not-being-in-a-world, however, gives us the perspective we need to see our usual being-in-the-world. "The *world as world* is disclosed first and foremost by anxiety" (Heidegger, 1962, 232/187). This is when the questions of existential crises press upon us – how did I get here? Is this really me? Is this really the life I want to live? In anxiety, "the totality of involvements of the ready-to-hand or present-at-hand discovered within-the-world, is, as such, of no consequence; it collapses ... completely lacking significance" (Heidegger, 1962, 231/186). This is horribly suffocating, but the crisis is also an opportunity to examine our lives and decide if this is really who we are and want to be, almost like an existential form of Husserl's transcendental bracketing.

Anxiety often comes on due to nothing in particular and drifts off for no reason. We usually return with relief to the mindless round of daily activities which keep us distracted and engaged, and try to forget all about the uncomfortable questions the mood put to us. However, we can instead take up those questions, perhaps deciding that in fact we do not like the self or the life that we have built for ourselves through the dozens of acts and decisions taken every day. This pause gives us the opportunity to start on a different path or we can go back to the old one but now as intentionally chosen rather than just falling in line with what one does.

Anxiety, along with the call of conscience and anticipation of death, make me realize that I have a limited time on this planet and that I need to stop coasting through life as one does. I need to take the reins and actively live my life:

> Dasein makes no choices, gets carried along by the nobody, and thus ensnares itself in inauthenticity. This process can be reversed only if Dasein specifically brings itself back to itself from its lostness in the "they".... "Making up" for not choosing signifies *choosing to make this choice* – deciding for a potentiality-for-Being, and making this decision from one's own Self. (Heidegger, 1962, 312–313/268)

This is at least part of resolute authenticity. There is a great deal of scholarly debate about just what this is, but it seems at least to be a way to exist excellently as what we are, at least somewhat like Aristotle's notion of flourishing.

Now we have a second, existential understanding of thinking and understanding to go with the practical mastery of tool-use. In Division I of *Being and Time*, to understand a tool was to use it competently: "interpretation is carried out primordially not in a theoretical statement but in an action of circumspective concern – laying aside the unsuitable tool" (Heidegger, 1962, 200/157). In Division II, to understand conscience's appeal is to make choices in full awareness of their nullity, of their ultimate groundlessness and unjustifiability: "understanding does not primarily mean just gazing at a meaning, but rather *understanding oneself in that potentiality*-for-Being which reveals itself in projection" (Heidegger, 1962, 307/263).

<u>Thinking Is Temporal.</u> Division I of *Being and Time* concludes by revealing care as the foundation of its initial definition of Dasein as being-in-the-world, then Division II uncovers temporality beneath that layer. This also departs from the tradition. Philosophers from Plato to Schopenhauer have looked to contemplation as a way to escape time, defining true knowledge as unchanging truths about that which does not itself change. According to an old view, a knower must share the properties of what they know in order to be able to make successful epistemological contact with it, so our ability to know eternal truths indicates a deep atemporality about ourselves, at least for our rational capacities.

Heidegger adheres to this principle of knower-known concordance but reverses it, resting it on timeliness instead of timelessness. We are trying to figure out the way to understand being by means of a study of our way of being as the understanding being.[15] Our existence has now been revealed to be at bottom temporality, so everything about us must be temporal, including our understanding.[16] The temporality of our understanding means that any meaning that we understand must be temporal, up to and including the meaning of being. We understand being temporally because our understanding works temporally. "If Dasein harbors the understanding of being within itself, and if temporality makes possible the Dasein in its ontological constitution, then *temporality* must also be the *condition of the possibility* of the *understanding of being*" (Heidegger, 1988, 280). Heidegger announced this on the first page of the book.[17]

Since each level of Dasein's existence makes the higher ones possible, finding temporality at the bottom means that everything above it – all that we are, do, and experience – occurs on the basis of time.

> We have given an Interpretation of some structures which are essential to Dasein's state-of-Being, and we have done so *before* exhibiting temporality, but with the aim of leading up to this. Our analysis of the temporality of concern has shown that these structures must be *taken back into temporality* existentially. (Heidegger, 1962, 421/370)

Along with the existential reinterpretation of structures of Division I, Division II also returns to those structures to give them a temporal reading.

Division I unpacked our understanding as knowing-how to use tools; now Division II shows how this is essentially conditioned by time. We are in-the-world by pursuing goals which by definition are not fully present, else we would not be working toward bringing them about. Thought temporally, goals are essentially futural – they are what we have not yet accomplished. This not-yet, however, is not a matter of simple nonexistence. As the force driving all of my actions, future goals are more present to me than the present – just with a different kind of presence. The very presence of a tool is already futural, for we grasp it in terms of what it *can*-do. Heidegger defines the being of a tool, readiness-to-hand, as an "in-order-to" which, he now explains, is what we might call a working-toward-something-to-come.

Among the tenses, Heidegger gives priority to the future since we only understand the past and present in light reflected back from the future. First,

---

[15] "Since the being of the world becomes comprehensible in the encounter, the understanding of the entity in itself is as such revealed only in a radical interpretation of Dasein" (Heidegger, 1985, 218).

[16] This is the main argument of Bill Blattner's influential *Heidegger's Temporal Idealism*.

[17] "Whenever Dasein tacitly understands and interprets something like Being, it does so with *time* as its standpoint. Time must be brought to light – and genuinely conceived – as the horizon for all understanding of Being and for any way of interpreting it. In order for us to discern this, *time needs to be explicated primordially as the horizon for the understanding of Being, and in terms of temporality as the Being of Dasein which understands Being*" (Heidegger, 1962, 39/17).

we can only understand anything at all because we are oriented towards the future. If we could not think about our goals, we would not seek them out and so would not do the activities that draw us into the world – hammering this nail now in-order-to bring the bookshelf into existence for-the-sake-of being a scholar. Second, our future goals determine what we think about by selectively training our attention on those aspects of the world relevant to our projects. Pursuing the goal of being a good professor, I enter a classroom with the intention to teach, and this task highlights certain instrumental chains as relevant – chalkboard, lectern – while leaving others unobtrusively in the background. These others – the electrical system – would be in the forefront for someone who entered the same room with different goals, such as an electrician. What we think about and how we think about gets retroactively set by these future-oriented thoughts.

While the tradition has taught us that only what is present and self-identical is truly real, Dasein is always "*ahead of itself* . . . 'beyond itself'" (Heidegger, 1962, 236/191). When I cross the room I'm already at the door, otherwise I would not get up in the first place nor know where to walk to. As we have seen, this understanding is not necessarily a thematic, theoretical understanding; our thinking of them is embodied in our actions.

Here we can see how Division II's two understandings of our way of being – the existential and the temporal – come together. All of our intelligent behavior is futural as we project the kind of person we seek to be. To be one of these roles or for-the-sakes-of-which such as a teacher or electrician means doing the relevant activities with the appropriate equipment in the right kinds of contexts. But since these activities are all teleological, they can only continue as long as they are not fulfilled. The point at which all requirements of a role have been fulfilled does not represent the moment when I truly and fully am that role, but rather the moment I stop being it. Being a student means doing all the activities that will eventually lead to graduation; that is the future goal which retroactively guides and organizes the time and actions of being a student. Since that is the culmination, as long as one is pursuing it one never purely and simply *is* it; being a student means always being on the way *toward* being a student. When you arrive at its culmination and walk across the stage, the second you take the diploma into your hand, you are no longer a student but a graduate – an ex-student. Thus, the traditional notion of understanding as basking in the presence of a completely present object of knowledge that stills our restless drives simply cannot fit an entity like Dasein. We are in-the-world like sharks in water – we keep moving forward, or we die. Heidegger's model of thinking accommodates this intrinsic "incompleteness," not as a flaw due to our finitude but as a necessary feature of the only kind of thinking we can engage in or even recognize. This fits his ontology which accommodates nonbeing into being, absence into presence, possibility into actuality, and the future into the present. "Any Dasein always exists in just such a manner that its 'not-yet' *belongs* to it" (Heidegger, 1962, 287/243).

However, while Heidegger prioritizes the future, the past plays an essential role. Authenticity requires us to decide for ourselves what for-the-sake-of-which we will choose, but these come from our society. This is the positive, constitutive role that society plays in *Being and Time*. There are no functions, roles, or actions set aside by reality or God as the ones we must properly do. Instead, they are made possible by the worldly scaffolding of our community, and only ones sanctioned and recognized in the public sphere are open to us. These do not come from nature either, but from history, the "more concrete working out of temporality" (Heidegger, 1962, 434/382). Thus, it is their culture's historical heritage that shapes the array of ways of being a human and living a life available to any individual Dasein and, as these for-the-sakes-of-which are what shape our thinking, people in different historical periods are going to think and see the world in fundamentally different ways.

Temporality is not made up of three tenses conjoined, or of moments that do not yet exist, are in the present, and then no longer exist. Rather, they are all intertwined in a way that each enables and makes sense of the others. This structure is also present in understanding.

> Dasein 'is' its past in the way of *its* own Being, which, to put it roughly, 'historizes' out of its future on each occasion. Whatever the way of being it may have at the time, and thus with whatever understanding of Being it may possess, Dasein has grown up both into and in a traditional way of interpreting itself: in terms of this it understands itself proximally and, within a certain range, constantly. By this understanding, the possibilities of its Being are disclosed and regulated. (Heidegger, 1962, 41/20)

Our past heritage offers us the future-oriented for-the-sakes-of-which which then make the past and present intelligible in a mutually enabling virtuous circle.

<u>Thinking Is Reflexive.</u> As we pointed out at the beginning of our discussion, the thinking that animates *Being and Time* is reflexive from the start in its attempt to understand understanding. The lessons that it learns apply to the process by which it learned them, as thinking is both the subject thought about and the subject thinking about it. The last quarter or so of the book argues that because Dasein is temporal and time takes the concrete form of history, everything about Dasein has to be historical. The never-published second part of *Being and Time* was going to apply this conclusion about the historicality of thinking to itself by tracing how Kant, Descartes, and Aristotle had thought of the relation between time and being.

Heidegger approaches the history of metaphysics with the insight that, as Nietzsche pointed out, time has always served metaphysics "as a criterion for distinguishing realms of Being" (Heidegger, 1962, 39/18). That which is in time has always been treated as less real than that which is timeless, a view Nietzsche attributes to weakness in dealing with change, whereas Heidegger sees its source in Dasein's inauthenticity. We are fundamentally temporal but we prefer to think of ourselves as thinking timeless thoughts about eternal subjects because, as in one of Plato's arguments for the immortality of the soul, that entails a timeless thinker (*Phaedo* 79 c-e).

Heidegger applies his analysis of conformism to the way ideas from the history of philosophy have surreptitiously infiltrated our ways of thinking so that we employ third-hand versions of Platonic or Aristotelian notions without even knowing it. Just as "proximally and for the most part, Dasein *is not itself*" and "Dasein makes no choices, gets carried along by the nobody" (Heidegger, 1962, 151/116; 312/268), so we generally think with other's thoughts.

> Dasein simultaneously falls prey to the tradition of which it has more or less explicitly taken hold. This tradition keeps it from providing its own guidance, *whether in inquiring or in choosing*. This holds true – and by no means least – for that understanding which is rooted in Dasein's ownmost Being, and for the possibility of developing it – namely, for ontological understanding. (Heidegger, 1962, 42–43/21, italics added)

As we inauthentically acquire an "addiction to becoming 'lived'" (Heidegger, 1962, 240/196), so too do we seek to be *thought through* rather than thinking things through for ourselves. Over time, these traditional ideas have "hardened" (Heidegger, 1962, 44/22) into clichés or truisms recited by rote that now hinder thought more than helping it. They cover over more than they uncover, leading us to see what we think we will see, rather than what actually shows up.

While these conventional concepts have generally permeated our thinking without our knowing it, we can bring this into the open.

> It is not necessary that in resoluteness one should *explicitly* know the origin of the possibilities upon which that resoluteness projects itself. It is rather in Dasein's temporality, and there only, that there lies any possibility that the existential potentiality-for-Being upon which it projects itself can be gleaned *explicitly* from the way in which Dasein has been traditionally understood. (Heidegger, 1962, 437/385)

Heidegger is taking up the age-old question of being that has reverberated throughout the history of philosophy and *"handing down explicitly"* (Heidegger, 1962, 437/385) this inquiry to himself, making it his own by asking it in a way appropriate to his situation and time in his *"reciprocative rejoinder"* (Heidegger, 1962, 438/386) to the tradition.

Heidegger's plans for the unpublished Part Two of *Being and Time* show how he has, in his terms, chosen his heroes.

> The authentic repetition of a possibility of existence that has been – the possibility that Dasein may choose its hero – is grounded existentially in anticipatory resoluteness; for it is in resoluteness that one first chooses the choice which makes one free for the struggle of loyally following in the footsteps of that which can be repeated. (Heidegger, 1962, 437/385)

His heroes are the philosophers who inspire his philosophical inquiry by, among other things, the seriousness with which they treated the now neglected question of being.

> The question we are touching upon is not just any question. It is one which provided a stimulus for the researches of Plato and Aristotle, only to subside from then on *as a theme for actual investigation*. What these two men achieved was to persist through many alterations and 'retouchings' down to the 'logic' of Hegel. And what they wrested with the utmost intellectual effort from the phenomena, fragmentary and incipient though it was, has long since become trivialized. (Heidegger, 1962, 21/2)

His reciprocative rejoinder is loyal to the spirit of their thinking while struggling with the letter in what he calls a "destruction" of the tradition. This doesn't mean smashing up traditional ideas but dismantling them carefully, studying how they were put together so that we can understand the original experiences that gave rise to them. This is a laborious and, for Heidegger, a deeply respectful, almost reverential activity, while remaining even for that reason continuously critical.

To apply Division I's tool model once more, our thoughtless use of these concepts needs some kind of a breakdown of them for us to become thematically and critically aware of our own presuppositions. Going through the history of philosophy as he planned to in Part Two (and we have smatterings of it in the published portions) would have done this, but there is another method vaguely intimated.

Anticipating philosopher of science Thomas Kuhn,[18] Heidegger says that sciences make incremental progress when their fundamental organizing notions are taken for granted, but "the real 'movement' of the sciences takes place when their basic concepts undergo a more or less radical revision which is transparent to itself" (Heidegger, 1962, 29/9). The revolutions that occur in times of "a crisis in its basic concepts" – one example he gives is relativity's profound revision of the nature of time and space – are the moments when sciences "put research on

---

[18] Heidegger's *The Question Concerning the Thing* gives a more detailed proto-Kuhnian account of science.

new foundations" (ibid.). These are the times when a discipline stops asking about these or those beings in standardly accepted ways to investigate their being and explore new ways of inquiry.

The sciences – the German word *"Wissenschaften"* has a much broader application than the English "sciences," as we can see from Heidegger's listing of history and theology as other examples (Heidegger, 1962, 30/10) – must philosophize or, as he will later say, "think" at these moments. Philosophy's business is to continuously rethink the deep nature and definitions of what is regarded as settled by other disciplines. This is what keeps philosophy fresh, and also keeps it from generating a consensus on established results. The problem is philosophy too can become "normal science," i.e., a plodding, unthinking application of taken-for-granted notions – inauthenticity for the discipline. "The real 'movement' of" *philosophy* also comes when *its* "basic concepts undergo a more or less radical revision which is transparent to itself" – which is precisely what *Being and Time* is attempting to bring about. It is revising standard understandings of time, space, selfhood, and many other fundamental notions and doing so transparently by explaining how and why it is doing it. Thus, not only does Heidegger consider his concepts better than the traditional ones, but their innovativeness by itself can create an awareness-inducing moment in philosophers who take standard notions for granted. Seeing alternatives breaks down the narrow range of concepts we had been restricting ourselves to. This large-scale destruction of the tradition is the breakdown needed to achieve authenticity in philosophizing.

Thinking Is Transcendental. Extraordinarily original, *Being and Time* is at the same time a brilliant synthesis of other philosophers, which fits with its views about the historicity of all thinking. Along with Kierkegaard and Aristotle (and dashes of Hegel, Nietzsche, and Dilthey), the main influences are Kant and Husserl. These two are transcendental idealists, which means that their work studies the way our thinking structures our experience.

Heidegger rejects both realism and idealism (though he rejects realism more [Heidegger, 1962, 251/207]), but many have found his early work to at least overlap transcendental philosophy in important ways.[19] Take his discussion of breakdowns, for instance. We are the ones who change-over the hammer's way of being from ready-to-hand to present-at-hand by disengaging use to just stare at it. "What we are talking about – the heavy hammer – shows itself differently ... because we are looking *at* the ready-to-hand thing which we encounter, and looking at it 'in a new way' as something present-at-hand. *The understanding*

---

[19] Some important works on this topic are Blattner, 1999; Braver, 2007; Carman, 2007; and Crowell and Malpas, 2007.

of Being by which our concernful dealings with entities within-the-world have been guided *has changed over*" (Heidegger, 1962, 412/361). The change-over in the entity's way of being is due to the change in our way of understanding its being that accompanies an alteration of our intelligent interactions with it.

This seems to place Dasein at the center and foundation of ontology, an insight Heidegger credits Kant with.

> The direction of the path [Kant] follows, by returning to the subject in its broadest sense, is the only one that is possible and correct. It is the direction of the interpretation of being, actuality, existence that was followed not just by modern philosophy since Descartes, by expressly orienting its philosophical problems to the subject ... or toward what is basically meant by it, namely, our Dasein (Heidegger, 1988, 73).

Heidegger does, of course, make significant alterations to Kant's project.

> If we radicalize the Kantian problem of ontological knowledge in the sense that we do not limit this problem to the ontological foundation of the positive sciences and if we do not take this problem as a problem of judgment but as the radical and fundamental question concerning the possibility of understanding being in general, then we shall arrive at the philosophically fundamental problematic of *Being and Time*. (Heidegger, 1997a, 289)

Heidegger radicalizes Kant by exploring multiple, active forms of thinking such as his pragmatic and existential understandings that go beyond the traditional exclusive focus on theoretical knowing. However, he gives credit to Kant for being the one who "for the first time, came upon this primordial productivity of the 'subject'" (Heidegger, 1984b, 210) where productivity means the way our thinking and acting determine the mode of being that entities have. It is these dippings into a subject-centered transcendental idealism, he will later say, that motivated him to change his thinking in the later phase of his career.

Part II Later Heidegger: Thoughtful Thinking

> We are compelled to follow the circle. This is neither a makeshift nor a defect. To enter upon this path is the strength of thought, to continue on it is the feast of thought, assuming that thinking is a craft.
>
> Heidegger, *Basic Writings: from Being and Time (1927) to The Task of Thinking (1964)*, 144

<u>Thinking Changes.</u> Heidegger's thinking and writing changed over the course of his career, though exactly how and how much is a matter of considerable debate among scholars. Most accept some degree of continuity and some degree of change but differ on their relative significance and ratio. His career is often divided between the early work – roughly 1919–1930 or so, often represented

(as here) by *Being and Time* – and the later – from about the early to mid-1930s to the end of his career, consisting generally in lecture courses and essays without any single representative work. While this division is simplistic – the later work in particular continued to develop and change – I find it hard to deny that a particularly sharp division did occur around 1930 which is often called *die Kehre* or the turn.

The unquestionable point of continuity lies in the question he never stopped asking. "Every thinker thinks only one thought" (Heidegger, 1968, 50) and Heidegger's one thought is the question of being – "*of all questions, both the most basic and the most concrete*" (Heidegger, 1962, 29/9). While he continued asking it throughout his career, it subtly changed in the asking – as is appropriate. "When thinking is addressed by an issue and then goes after this, it can happen that it changes along the way" (Heidegger, 2012a, 108).

Being and Time addresses being in terms of the ontological difference, the fundamental distinction between (1) beings – the various entities we encounter and interact with in various ways – and (2) being – their mode or way of being. These modes aren't too far from the traditional notion of essence, though more dynamic: things actively are or behave in certain ways which sets the range of actions it is appropriate for us to take with them. Perhaps the main point of the book as we have it is to correct our tendency to interpret the two most common kinds of being – tools' readiness-to-hand and Dasein's existence – inappropriately (*uneigentlich*). The tradition has recognized presence-at-hand as the only legitimate mode of being, so it forces all of our thinking about the great variety of beings into that one mold. This can be seen as an adaptation of his teacher Husserl's regional ontology. Husserl held that instead of reducing all of reality to a single form of being real, we should recognize and explore fundamentally heterogeneous types of beings that act and interact in fundamentally divergent ways.

Heidegger expands this project in his later work, acknowledging more beings such as artworks, technology, and homes that require their own concepts and terminology if we are to avoid conflating them with others. But he also, in my view, adds a third "layer" to the ontological difference, one that only makes a brief appearance in *Being and Time* but becomes centrally important to his later work – being itself (or the truth of being, *Seyn*, the clearing, or the "there is," all roughly equivalent). This "level" indicates that which is most difficult for us to become aware of – awareness itself, the sheer fact that beings show themselves to us in some way or other. In this later tripartite ontological difference, as with the early two-part one, the layers or facets (there is no good word for them, as Heidegger often points out) are essentially intertwined and interdependent – "Being is always the Being of a being" – while also being radically different from each other – "the Being of beings 'is' not itself a being" (Heidegger, 1962, 29/9, 26/6, translations slightly altered).

One of the central mechanisms driving *Being and Time* was the way breakdowns disrupt smooth operations, thereby making them conspicuous. Previously invisible tools suddenly stick out when they break down, which can light up the world made up of their interlinked chains, with the ultimate culmination in the life we make of ourselves in that world breaking down in an existentialist state of anxiety. The later work applies a version of this mechanic to the ontological difference, showing how each level conceals or covers over the others. We experience (1) various beings in terms of (2) the kind of being that they are (using tools, examining objects, talking with people), but we're so absorbed in interacting with the beings that we rarely think about their mode of being. I never contemplate what it means to be a shoe or equipmentality in general when putting on my shoes or taking a walk, though my appropriate use of them demonstrates my preontological understanding of it. Explicitly examining these (2) modes of being is what metaphysicians do as they try to define what it means to be a being, but both their examination of (2) beingness and the everyday use of (1) beings hide the most basic fact that (3) anything is manifest to us at all. We pay no attention to that in our daily business, and Heidegger argues that metaphysical explanations actually end up concealing it, leaving it the most inconspicuous phenomenon of all – the phenomenon of phenomenality.

Being and Time moved our thinking from level (1) to (2) by giving us detailed analyses of three (2) modes of being (objects' presence-at-hand, tools' readiness-to-hand, and Dasein's existence). The main goal of Heidegger's later work on the other hand is to draw our attention to level (3), this ever-hidden-because-always-present fact of awareness. This is when "the clearing belonging to the essence of Being suddenly clears itself and lights up . . . . It brings itself into its own brightness . . . . The essence, the coming to presence, of Being enters into its own emitting of light" (Heidegger, 1977, 44–45). This completes thinking's inherent reflexivity, its intrinsic tendency to think of thinking, by creating a phenomenology of phenomenology. However, it proves extraordinarily difficult to do. Our concepts and language are primarily suited to dealing with (1) beings, and have been augmented by centuries of metaphysics to address (2) beingness, but (3) being itself has been ignored or forgotten throughout the history of philosophy – it has always been utterly inconspicuous. Hence Heidegger's fifty-year, 100+-volume struggle to say what is nearest and most simple, trying to get us to think fully about what it means to think and how we are getting thought to.

Thinking through Nihilism. Heidegger often harbors suspicion of taken-for-granted divisions, preferring holistic interconnections in general. Just as he does not separate emotions from thinking, neither does he want to distinguish between practical and theoretical thinking, at least not for the kind of thinking he's talking about. "Such thinking is neither theoretical nor practical. It comes to pass before this distinction. Such thinking is, insofar as it is, recollection of Being and nothing else. Belonging to Being, because thrown by Being into the preservation of its truth and claimed for such preservation, it thinks Being" (Heidegger, 1993a, 259). His analyses teach us a lot about the nature of thought, but always in service to a goal that could be characterized as ethical in the broadest sense of a term. "If the name 'ethics,' in keeping with the basic meaning of the word *ethos*, should now say that 'ethics' ponders the abode of man, then that thinking which thinks the truth of Being as the primordial element of man, as one who ek-sists, is in itself the original ethics" (Heidegger, 1993a, 258). Since what it means to be a human (a word he uses more than Dasein in the later work) is to think being, we can only understand what it is to live appropriately by understanding how thinking works and what it is to do it with excellence (to once again use an Aristotelian argument). One way to understand his ethics of thinking is to place it in relation to the philosopher Heidegger considers to be the thinker of our times, Nietzsche.

Heidegger agrees with Nietzsche's diagnosis of our time as one of nihilism, which Heidegger understands as a kind of homelessness, of not being at home in this world. His early work presents existential homelessness as endemic to the human condition. This emerges most forcefully in uncanniness or "*Unheimlichkeit*" – literally not-being-at-homeness, which uncovers the fact that there is no role "which belongs to existence" (Heidegger, 1962, 393/343), no true occupation that we are meant for that will make our lives meaningful. As dreadful as this realization is, "one is liberated in such a way that for the first time one can authentically understand and choose among the factical possibilities lying ahead," which gives Dasein "the possibility of taking over from itself its ownmost Being, and doing so of its own accord" (Heidegger, 1962, 308/263–264). The three existential experiences of Division II (anxiety, death, conscience) cut off the self-evident inertia our actions accumulate so that we can choose our roles deliberately. Thus, "resoluteness constitutes the loyalty of existence to its own Self. As resoluteness which is ready for anxiety, this loyalty is at the same time a possible way of revering the sole authority which a free existing can have" (Heidegger, 1962, 443/391). We have been thrown into this world, abandoned to a homelessness, and it is up to us to make one for ourselves.

The later work considers homelessness a historical rather than intrinsic condition. We live in a destitute age from which the god has fled. This view is closer to Nietzsche's analysis of nihilism as a historical phenomenon that results from the intrinsic development of certain philosophical and religious ideas. Nietzsche blames Platonism and Christianity while Heidegger sees the main culprit as modernity's focus on subjectivity.[20] Subjects are essentially self-standing, isolated from communities and world, which then become objects–things outside of us thrown-up-against us. As self-sufficient, we should aspire to complete control of ourselves, in particular of our thinking.

Descartes' *Meditations* attempt to make up for the misfortune of having once been young, since in that period he did not responsibly and actively examine beliefs but swallowed them down carelessly. He rectifies that error by beginning his epistemological life over again, starting from scratch so that he can in a sense give birth to himself, but this time the right way – as a mature adult who will believe responsibly from the start. This is possible since we enjoy an omnipotence over our will and thinking unlike anything else in our lives: "nothing lies entirely within our power except our thoughts" (Descartes/ ed. Cottingham et al., 2013, 123). Indeed, this power over our thinking is how we most resemble God and it is the key to how we shall "make ourselves, as it were, the lords and masters of nature" (ibid., 142–143). Kant insists that only a reason that is entirely spontaneous, unaffected by anything outside of itself, can be considered rational, much less free: "reason must regard itself as the author of its principles independent of foreign influences" just to count as reason at all (Kant, 2010, 50/448). Exerting influence on our thought processes makes something a cause, not a reason, which then compromises both practical freedom and theoretical rationality. Our task is to become autonomous by listening to ourselves alone to hear the law which is only "valid for us as men, since it has sprung from our will as intelligence and hence from our proper self" (Kant, 2010, 60/461). Nietzsche tells us that once traditional values have lost their value, we must create new ones for ourselves. This emphasis on autonomy does not make him the bad boy of metaphysics but rather the final step in its logical progression. "In Nietzsche's doctrine of the will to power as the 'essence' of all reality, the modern metaphysics of subjectity is completed" (Heidegger, 2002b, 178).

These three are representative of philosophers' attempts to get around or reclaim all of the passivity we find in ourselves, resenting any cognition we suffer rather than enact. We must do the thinking ourselves for it to be our thought, for it to be thought at all. We must initiate our thinking and liberate ourselves, for freedom merely given is not truly free. "What is decisive [in modernity as opposed to previous epochs] is that man specifically takes up this

---

[20] Heidegger does at times locate the seeds of modern subjectivity and so nihilism in ancient philosophy. See Braver 2007, 291–306.

position as one constituted by himself.... Man makes depend on himself the way he is to stand to beings as the objective. What begins is that mode of human being which occupies the realm of human capacity as the domain of measuring and execution for the purpose of the mastery of beings as a whole" (Heidegger, 2002b, 69).

Being and Time, however, insists on our thrownness. This means that Dasein "has been brought into its 'there', but not of its own accord.... It never comes back behind its thrownness in such a way that it might first release this 'that-it-is-and-has-to-be' from its Being-its-Self and lead it into the 'there'.... 'Being-a-basis' means never to have power over one's ownmost Being from the ground up" (Heidegger, 1962, 329–330/284). We were "thrown" into this life and our selves, not by our doing and or choice. We did not decide to be born, or where or when or as what; we did not enact our own creation nor can we stage a genuine self–re-creation. We breathe our first breath indebted to people and events that we had no part in, even though we owe our very existence and selfhood to them. This indebtedness – another way to translate guilt (*"Schuld"*) – is the existential underside of Heidegger's phrase, "always already."

Being and Time balances thrownness against our active thinking and projection of roles and activities, awarding some favor to the latter as futural, the tense which Heidegger considers first among equals. His later work, with its extreme emphasis on history and tradition, tips the scales back toward our situatedness in opposition to the modern focus on autonomous choice. Let's look at two arguments against modernity's view of thinking.

First, Heidegger finds it inaccurate and incoherent. Thinking cannot be active all the way down; without any influence from the objects of judgment we would have nothing to base our judgments on. "Thinking is no self-mastering activity encapsulated in itself nor a self-propelled toy. Thinking remains from the outset referred to what is to be thought; it is called by this" (Heidegger, 2012a, 145). When we talk about something, we say "the sorts of things that are suggested by what is addressed ... what the addressed allows to radiate of itself" (Heidegger, 1993a, 409). Any attempt to start constructing rationality from scratch is in principle impossible since in order to advance a single step, we need principles of thinking which, per hypothesis, have not been established at that point.

> The fundamental principles [of thought] cannot be proven. Indeed, every proof is already an act of thinking. The proof therefore already stands under the laws of thought. How could it presume to place itself above these in order to first justify their truth? ... Whenever we try to bring the basic principles of thinking before us they ineluctably become the topic of our thinking – and of

its laws. Every time, the laws of thinking already stand behind us, behind our back, so to speak, and guide every step of our reflections concerning them. (Heidegger, 2012a, 78)

We can never catch up with our thinking to "release this 'that-it-is-and-has-to-be' from its Being-its-Self." Our thinking rides the wave of a fundamental thrownness into thinking at all as well as thinking in certain ways. Any attempt to evaluate or alter it as a whole from the bottom up would itself take place on the basis of a way of thinking that would itself remain unquestioned and unexamined in the process.

We are indebted to being for being thrown into the ability to think; we are determined to reason. "This quest for reasons pervades human cognition even before it bothers with the founding of statements.... Without exactly knowing it, in some manner we are constantly addressed by, summoned to attend to, grounds and reasons" (Heidegger, 1996a, 3). This groundlessness would make thought viciously circular were we trying to enter it from outside – if, that is, starting from nothing, we had to justify the principle of seeking reasons and a particular way of doing so. Fortunately, being has "graced" us by "throwing" us into this circle of thought from the beginning. We are always already underway in questioning, enabled to think and act by the gift of irremediable heteronomy, relieving us of the impossible need for a rational baptism into rationality.

This also fits a phenomenological description of what happens when we think. "Such thoughts do not first come to be by way of mortal thinking. Rather our mortal thinking is always summoned by that thought to correspond to it or renounce it. We human beings do not come upon thoughts; thoughts rather come to us mortals" (Heidegger, 1996a, 53). We reach conclusions because certain notions reach out to us, suggesting themselves and pulling us toward them. What is great about the great thinkers and poets is not their creativity conceived of as Romantic geniuses but their sensitivity. They tune into and articulate the understanding of being that forms and informs the thinking and acting of their epoch. "What is great and constant in the thinking of a thinker simply consists in its expressly giving word to what always already resounds" (Heidegger, 1996a, 24). Nietzsche, in whom "the uprising of modern humanity into the absolute domination of subjectivity within the subjectivity of beings is fulfilled" (Heidegger, 2002b, 168), came to his views because features such as flux and conflict *stood out* to him, *striking* him as prominent. He *found* the need to create our values to be valuable, he didn't create that. "Nietzsche's thought has to plunge into metaphysics because Being radiates its own essence as will to power" (Heidegger, 1979, vol IV, 181). This is true generally: "we will have to rely on Being, and on how Being strikes our thinking, to ascertain from it what features essentially occur" (Heidegger, 1979, vol IV, 214). Thus Nietzsche, the great philosopher of will and creativity, "neither made nor chose his way himself, no more than any other thinker ever did. He is sent on his way."[21]

Heidegger's second argument is that modern subjectivity brings on nihilism. Nietzsche employs it to defeat nihilism but, ironically, "what was supposed to be the overcoming is but the completion of nihilism" (Heidegger, 2002b, 193). Nietzsche defines nihilism as the state in which "*the highest values devaluate themselves*. The aim is lacking; 'why?' finds no answer" (Nietzsche, 1968, §2, quoted at Heidegger, 2002b, 166). The highest Western values so far, those of Platonist Christianity, undermine themselves since the truthfulness it insists on ultimately leads believers to concede the dishonesty of their faith. The death of God creates nihilism by clearing away the old, objective values, but this nihilism also clears the way for those who are strong enough to create their own thoughts and values, ones more suited to embodied, mortal, earthly humans. The fact that we no longer *find* meaning in our lives gives us the opportunity to *put* meaning into them.

Heidegger sees this solution to nihilism as pouring gasoline on the fire by applying our contemporary technological attitude to values and purposes, that is, seeing it as a problem that is in our power to fix. "If we merely attempt, on our own authority, to set or seize upon the measure, then it becomes measureless and disintegrates into nothingness" (Heidegger, 1996b 167). As he succinctly puts it, "no one dies for mere values" (Heidegger, 2002b, 77). Nothing made by us can give us a true responsibility or place us under an obligation, nor can it connect us to anything larger than ourselves and our desires because there can be nothing beyond ourselves. "Beings *are*, yet they remain abandoned by Being and left to themselves, so as to be mere objects of our contrivance. All goals beyond men and peoples are gone" (Heidegger, 1994a, 159–160). Nietzsche defines the initial phase of weak nihilism as the strongest values so far devaluing themselves, while Heidegger sees in Nietzsche's own strong creative nihilism the very notion of value devaluing itself. Nietzsche's attempt to salvage it creates a situation where nothing can have genuine worth.

> Precisely through the characterization of something as "a value" what is so valued is robbed of its worth. That is to say, by the assessment of something as a value what is valued is admitted only as an object for man's estimation. But what a thing is in its Being is not exhausted by its being an object, particularly

---

[21] Heidegger, 1968, 46. Of course, Nietzsche being Nietzsche, there are plenty of passages that argue against this depiction of him and instead for a view much closer to Heidegger's. E.g., "I will not stop emphasizing a tiny little fact that these superstitious men are loath to admit: that a thought comes when 'it' wants, and not when 'I' want" (Nietzsche, 2001a, §17).

> when objectivity takes the form of value. Every valuing, even where it values positively, is a subjectivizing. It does not let beings: be. Rather, valuing lets beings: be valid – solely as the objects of its doing . . . . Thinking in values is the greatest blasphemy imaginable against Being. (Heidegger, 1993a, 251)

God might be dead but we can still blaspheme; this implies that some possibility of the sacred may survive as well.

Heidegger agrees with Nietzsche that nothing can guide us the way nature or reason or God used to. We both know too much and doubt too much to be able to find anything imbued with simple holiness, to follow any entity as absolutely authoritative. As Nietzsche's madman put it, we may still go to church but our prayers can never be anything more than Requiems for God. "The plight of the lack of a sense of plight will strike up against the remaining absent of both the advent *and* the absconding of the gods. This remaining absent is all the more uncanny the longer churches and forms of divine service survive (and seem permanent) and yet are unable to ground an original truth" (Heidegger, 2012b, 187/§120). However, even though the death of God has removed the possibility of a transcendent being saving us, the ontological difference teaches us that we are not faced only with beings; there is also being. Heidegger rebuts Sartre's humanistic voluntarism – "We are precisely in a situation where there are only human beings" – with this appeal – "We are precisely in a situation where principally there is Being" (Heidegger, 1993a, 237).

Nietzsche believed he reversed nihilism by celebrating instead of dreading the absence of values, while Heidegger sees this as its intensification. Instead of going back to some-thing that can supply values, he agrees that nothing can do so – but points out that, in fact, no-thing *can* do so.[22] This would be true nihil-ism because it sees meaningfulness coming from that which is nothing: since level (1) and (2) categorizations are so utterly incommensurable with (3) being itself, it does not show up within those categories as anything. It is not a being, no thing, nothing just as much as something. Clearing away *all* beings as potential sources or foundations for values opens our eyes to what is already there. We are in-the-world, but instead of a webwork of instrumental relations spread out by our chosen roles this now means that we walk "those paths and relations in which birth and death, disaster and blessing, victory and disgrace, endurance and decline acquire the shape of destiny for human being. The all-governing expanse of this open relational context is the world of this historical people" (Heidegger, 1993a, 167).

Heidegger finds meaningfulness even within this contemporary meaninglessness, for even meaninglessness makes sense to us and so makes sense for us. We find the modern project of autonomous self-creation intelligible, self-evidently valuable, even though the ancient Greeks probably would have found it

---

[22] For more on this, see Braver 2024b.

unintelligible and the medievals sinfully hubristic. While Heidegger finds this way of thinking about the world deeply problematic, it is still a thinking of the world, hence it is something we could not have created ourselves but to which we owe our ability to think, act, feel, exist. "'On one's own initiative' is already indicative of a way in which being itself lets human beings be in their essence" (Heidegger, 1996b, 90). Our modern quest to cut ourselves off from tradition is itself bequeathed to us by, as we have seen, the tradition of Descartes, Kant, and Nietzsche. "All philosophical discussion, even the most radical attempt to begin all over again, is pervaded by traditional concepts" (Heidegger, 1988, 22).

We are given meaning and significance just as we are given the perception of and urge to strive after reasons. We receive "from Being itself the assignment of those directives that must become law and rule for man .... Only such dispatching is capable of supporting and obligating. Otherwise all law remains merely something fabricated by human reason" (Heidegger, 1993a, 262). Instead of resenting this groundlessness since reason ultimately rests on nothing, we should be grateful that it gives us this motivation in a way that, as Nietzsche showed, no being can, giving thanks for nothing. The world abounds in ethical significance, as Levinas explores in his phenomenology-inspired work, and we cannot help but be open to it as our relation to being is the ultimate always already. We are not homeless; we belong. We belong to and with being because we are of being; we are essentially with-being or in-the-clearing the way Dasein is with-others or in-the-world. Learning to think, the project we have been involved in, is not leaping "into an abyss" but is rather "a curious, indeed unearthly thing that we must first leap onto the soil on which we really stand" (Heidegger, 1968, 41). We find it difficult because we tend to think ourselves apart from being, leaving us unprepared to think of ourselves as a thinking part of being. "Every way of thinking *takes its way* already *within* the total relation of Being and man's nature, or else it is not thinking at all (Heidegger, 1968, 80). We need to appreciate the fact that even nihilism is a world gifted to us. Despite the negative ways he depicts contemporary technological understanding, he also insists that "even in positionality as an essential destiny of being there essences a light from the flash of beyng" (Heidegger, 2012a, 71).

Thinking Is Wondrous. In *Being and Time* Heidegger states that Dasein is thrown. No one and nothing threw us here for no purpose, we are abandoned to make our own way and our own home without direction or directions. As he often does, Heidegger takes up this theme in his later work but gives it a new significance.

> Man is rather 'thrown' from Being itself into the truth of Being, so that ek-sisting in this fashion he might guard the truth of Being, in order that beings might appear in the light of Being as the beings they are .... Man is the shepherd of Being. (Heidegger, 1993a, 234)

Before, there was no possibility of a special way to live that was set out for us which would enable us to fulfill our essence and true purpose. There was no for-the-sake-of-which "which belongs to existence" (Heidegger, 1962, 393/343) – i.e., written into our very being – but now he finds one. This comes out in the word "existence," the early term for Dasein's (2) being, in that its etymology signifies a standing-outside ourselves that opens us up to our relatedness to being.

> What is Da-sein, and what does it mean to "exist" [*existieren*]? Da-sein is the enduring of the truth of beyng, and Dasein "is" this, and only this, as an ex-sisting [*ex-sistierend*] self which steadfastly withstands exposedness . . . . 'For the sake of itself,' i.e., purely as preservation and stewardship of being, provided what is fundamentally essential is indeed the understanding of being. (Heidegger, 2012b, 238–239/§178)

Since we are the revealer – the being who, by standing out in the open, enables beings to manifest themselves – we are charged with the "duty" of revealing being in the most careful and attentive way possible. Taking up our ability to let beings appear, celebrating it gratefully, and giving beings the kind of care-ful attention that lets them appear most fully would be projecting the openness that we are thrown into. "The opening up of the open region, and the clearing of beings, happens only when the openness that makes its advent in thrownness is projected" (Heidegger, 1993a, 196). We reveal beings most when we think them, and we reveal this revelation in thinking it.

Thrownness takes on new significance due to the importance that we understand that this is not our action, done on our initiative. "Everything depends on our inhering in this clearing that is propriated by Being itself – never made or conjured by ourselves. We must overcome the compulsion to lay our hands on everything" (N, 1979 vol III, 181). That is how thought is presented by transcendental thought, a notion his early work at least flirted with.

> The carrying out of the projection of the truth of beyng, in the sense of an entering into the open realm such that the projector of the projection experiences himself as thrown, i.e., as appropriated by beyng. The opening accomplished by the projection is an opening only if it occurs as an experience of thrownness and thus of belonging to beyng. That is what makes it essentially distinct from all merely *transcendental* modes of knowledge regarding conditions of possibility. (Heidegger, 2012b, 188–189/§122)

To think of thought transcendentally parallels thinking of values as projected by our will which forever keeps us from discovering our essence as the thinker of being.

> Man . . . is continually approaching the brink of the possibility of pursuing and promulgating nothing but what is revealed in ordering, and of deriving all his standards on this basis. Through this the other possibility is blocked – that man

> might rather be admitted sooner and ever more primally to the essence of what is unconcealed and to its unconcealment, in order that he might experience as his essence the requisite belonging to revealing. (Heidegger, 1993a, 331)

Thrownness has now become givenness, the gift of being able to reveal beings in various ways – thinking about them, poeticizing them, interacting with them. Our attitude should be one of gratitude for what we've been given, not pride in what we have done.

We give thanks for the ability to think by thinking, our way of participating in the self-revelation of being. We are midwives to arguments, as Socrates said, because reasons emanate from all around us. The world provokes us to reason about it, appearing as question-able and question-worthy, as in need of and suited to reasons. Thinking and speaking beings brings them forth to show themselves in thoughts and words. Our unique response-ability gives us a unique responsibility; as the only beings who can let being be by bringing it to manifestation, we have an obligation to do so as fully as possible.

To think gratefully for being's graciousness is to wonder. Wondering why enables us to wonder at the fact that we can wonder why, unlike animals, plants, and rocks. "Of all beings, only the human being, called upon by the voice of being, experiences the wonder of all wonders: that beings are" (Heidegger, 1998b, 234). All philosophy is born of wonder and what is more wondrous than that we can be struck by wonder at all and, reciprocally, that there is something to wonder at? Heidegger wants us to see the beauty in the fact that we see beauty, to love loving, to be thankful for our capacity for thankfulness, all of which comes from being be-ing. The ultimate inconspicuousness of being means that "one can no longer be struck by the miracle of beings: that they are" (Heidegger, 1994a, 169). This is another wonder enacted by no-thing. The existence of all that is can *only* be miraculous *without* God, for Her existence would supply a straightforward explanation: the creator God created. It is far more mysterious, wondrous, gratitude-inducingly gratuitous if nothing is responsible for it, and no-thing is. Although there is no one or thing to be grateful to, that enhances rather than prevents our gratitude, the "thanks that alone pays homage to the grace that being has bestowed upon the human essence in thinking" (Heidegger, 1998b, 236). This essential openness by thinking being is what shows us that we are not homeless.

> Man's distinctive feature lies in this, that he, as the being who thinks, is open to Being, face to face with Being; thus man remains referred to Being and so answers to it.... A belonging to Being prevails within man, a belonging which listens to Being because it is appropriated to Being. (Heidegger, 2002a, 31)

This mutual appropriation is our authenticity, our being-at-home, our special function and the source of all meaning. Our quest is to let being be.

Our belonging is as pervasive as anything can be, yet we pass over it as the deepest always already. "We do not reside sufficiently as yet where in reality we already are" (ID 33). Where smoothly functioning tools were inconspicuous in the early work, being is "the most inconspicuous of inconspicuous things, the simplest of simple things, the nearest of things near and most remote of things remote, among which we mortals reside all our lives" (Heidegger, 1993a, 415). (3) Being is the manifestation of (1) beings in their (2) ways of being but it directs our attention away from the sheer event of manifestation to what gets manifested. The very unconcealment of them conceals itself. "If we stand in a clearing in the woods, we see only what can be found within it: the free place, the trees about – and precisely not the luminosity of the clearing itself" (Heidegger, 1994a, 178).

Thus we still need some kind of interruption, which can bear a resemblance to what served that function in *Being and Time*. "The essentialization of truth will be attained only if the usual everyday way of being human is successfully dislocated, as it were, and is then allowed to settle on its proper ground" (Heidegger, 1994a, 179–180). One form of the breakdown of our thinking that can make it conspicuous comes in unanswerable questions. Wonder, the inspiration of philosophy since Plato and Aristotle, wonders why the universe is but no explanation can fully account for it. Anything used to explain will itself be something that is and so need explaining in turn, thus creating a *reductio ad infinitum*. This baffling dead-end of inquiry, however, need not be seen as a failure but an opening up of new dimensions. The shock to the systematic explanations of reality can turn us toward the simple mystery of what is the presence of what is present to us. This end to philosophy can supply a new end for thinking.

> This basic disposition of shocked and diffident restraint resonate in the essential human being ... establishes ... the opening of the simplicity and greatness of beings and the originally compelled necessity of securing in beings the truth of beyng so as to *give the historical human being a goal once again*, namely, to become the one who grounds and preserves the truth of beyng, to be the "there" as the ground required by the very essence of beyng, or, in other words, to care. That is what care means .... *Care is uniquely "for the sake of beyng"* – *not of the beyng of the human being* but of the beyng of beings as a whole.[23]

---

[23] Heidegger, 2012b, 15/§5, all italics added; my thanks to Richard Polt for the sake of bringing this passage to my attention.

This is his redefinition of *Being and Time*'s second definition of Dasein – care – but now it is being that we care about by caring for it.

Knowledge shuts down wonder since we no longer have to wonder when we know the answer. It is the unanswerable questions that can provoke an unending wonder.

> We know too much and believe too readily ever to feel at home in a questioning which is powerfully experienced. For that we need the ability to wonder at what is simple, and to take up that wonder as our abode . . . . Thoughtful wonder speaks in questioning. (Heidegger, 1984a, 104)

This unsatisfiable intellectual wondering *about* turns into an awed wondering *at*, an astonishment at the mere fact that anything is at all and that we can experience anything at all.

Grateful wonder cherishes our ability to think being, to see and know and speak. The great celebrators are the artists and thinkers, for they are the ones who are most aware of the favor they have been granted. They engage in these abilities to the utmost – painting as the celebration of being able to see, music the fact that we can hear, poetry that we speak and philosophy that the world yields itself to our thoughts. Heidegger wants us to think thoughtfully and thankfully, which means being aware that awareness is a gift, a view not possible for autonomy-driven modernity. "The things for which we owe thanks are not things we have from ourselves . . . . But the thing given to us . . . is thinking . . . . How can we give thanks for this endowment, the gift of being able to think?" (Heidegger, 1968, 142–143). Instead of taking it for granted, we should take it as granted to us.

Thinking Is *Really* Historical. Heidegger's early account presents history's role in our existence as important but limited. While the for-the-sakes-of-which and their concomitant tools come from historically varying cultures, the formal structure of Dasein's being appears to remain the same for everyone at all times and places (suggested, e.g., at Heidegger, 1962, 38/17). An eighth-century itinerant monk's shoes will withdraw from his notice during prayer the same way mine do while writing a book on Heidegger because we both have the same mode of being – existence – as do the shoes – readiness-to-hand. The second part of *Being and Time* was going to turn explicitly to the history of philosophy, but as a tale of deep continuity which relegates historical development to a matter of relatively superficial variations. "Kant took over Descartes' position quite dogmatically" (Heidegger, 1962, 45/24), while "what presents itself in Descartes' case is . . . no break, but instead a process of seizing upon a prefigured possibility . . . that Greek philosophy specified" (Heidegger, 2005, 83), with the result that "Kant's basic ontological orientation remains that of the Greeks" (Heidegger, 1962, 49/26).

Where his early work explores three modes of Being that appear to remain stable across history, Heidegger's later work sees beings as having a more uniform metaphysical nature within a historical period. Each epoch has a specific way in which beings appear which sets determinate parameters to what thoughts will strike people as sensible at that time. He variously calls an epoch's conception of what is real its clearing, understanding of Being, truth, or sending of Being. Each period has a specific understanding of what it means to be that founds and shapes all human thought, practice, and discourse at that time. "The fundamental characteristic of all beings ... must, so to speak, be 'encountered' by the thinking of this thought in every region of beings: in nature, art, history, politics, in science and in knowledge in general" (Heidegger, 1979, vol III, 19). The Greeks understood beings as spontaneously emerging nature (*physis*), the medievals saw beings as divine creations, moderns think of them as scientifically knowable objects, and we today find only resources to be technologically manipulated to satisfy our needs and desires. Instead of the change-over in mode of being occurring when Dasein stops using and starts staring at something or vice versa, these epochal shifts are historical change-overs of modes of being which is why "thinking is intrinsically historical" (Heidegger, 2012b, 187/§120). Whereas the early work founded the study of being on the examination of Dasein's existential structure, now thinking of being means examining "the changing forms in which Being shows itself epochally and historically" (Heidegger, 1972, 52).

Neither being nor thinking can be separated from each other, nor from the history of philosophy which documents how those most sensitive to the reverberations of thought have put their epoch's understanding of being into words. Studying metaphysical texts calls our attention to the multiplicity of clearings there have been. Their incommensurability means that none can absorb or account for the others, revealing the contingency of each way of understanding being, including our own. While none can claim absolute universal truth, each reveals beings for a time which makes them true for their epoch, despite their incompatibility with each other.

> This foundation happened in the West for the first time in Greece .... The realm of beings thus opened up was then transformed into a being in the sense of God's creation. This happened in the Middle Ages. This kind of being was again transformed at the beginning and during the course of the modern age. Beings became objects that could be controlled and penetrated by calculation .... At each time there happened unconcealment of beings. (Heidegger, 1993a, 201)

As a responding and co-responding to being, thinking is always historically situated. "If we represent thinking as a universal human capacity then it becomes an imaginary construction" (Heidegger, 2012a, 89). There is no metaphysical realm or noumenal self that could harbor transcendent ideas or rules beyond the vicissitudes of time and everything human-all-too-human. We are thrown inescapably into history, which means into a particular historical epoch. "Every sort of thought, however, is always only the execution and consequence of a mode of historical Dasein, of the fundamental position taken towards Being and toward the way in which beings are manifest as such, i.e. toward truth" (Heidegger, 1993a, 294–295).

Heidegger defines our contemporary way of thinking and being as technology. He does not mean the various electronic gadgets we use to make our lives easier, however, but the equip-mentality that leads us to create them, which he calls the essence of technology. Whereas the former are things we make, the latter is in principle something that we cannot and could not have made. We saw earlier his phenomenological and ethical arguments for the receptivity of thinking; here is his logical argument.

The essence of technology means seeing the world in terms of, on the one hand, problems, inconveniences, and obstacles to getting what we want, and resources we can use to take care of those issues on the other. Thinking that you can create this way of thinking is self-contradictory because it presupposes this very frame of mind. You must already be looking at things technologically in order to think about thinking as an inefficient tool that needs to be improved.

> Long before the end of the eighteenth century, when the first machines were invented and set running in England, positionality, the essence of technology, was already afoot in a concealed manner. This says: the essence of technology already reigned beforehand, so much so that it first of all lit up the region within which the invention of something like power-producing machines could at all be sought out and attempted. (Heidegger, 2012a, 32–33)

Our understanding of being is what lays out the options that strike us as reasonable and plausible, the range of thoughts that occur to us, so we can only act technologically if we already think technologically. We will only look around for raw materials to put together in useful ways if things show up as problems to be solved with the right tools. All of our actions are reactions to the way the world solicits us to act. However, thinking technologically, which Heidegger sometimes calls calculative thought, is not the only option for thinking, as I will show in what follows.

We can apply this analysis to Descartes and Nietzsche, Heidegger's bookends of modern philosophy. Descartes was dissatisfied with the education he received because, among other things, medieval theology could not help us make devices that improve our lives. He set out to reprogram his own mind, rebooting it and then rewriting his ways of thinking from scratch in ways that were more conducive to making technological advances. As he describes one of his most important works, he was seeking a "method of rightly conducting reason and seeking the truth in the sciences" where the "and" means "in order to" (Descartes/ed. Cottingham et al, 6). Heidegger points out that such a move cannot but come too late. To even consider such a project, Descartes had to already have been thinking about his own thinking as a tool that should be brought up to optimal efficiency in order to get what he wants – science which could make technology. Being motivated by this solution could only occur to someone who views the world as problems in need of solutions. A devout medieval peasant, for instance, would not see illness as a matter of inconvenience and discomfort to be assuaged with a little effort and ingenuity, but as a just punishment handed down by a righteous God which it is his duty to suffer with patience, dignity, and grace.

Whereas Descartes came too late, Nietzsche's project necessarily occurs too soon (as the madman says of his announcement of the death of God, "'I come too early', he then said; 'my time is not yet'" (Nietzsche, 2001b, §125). His attempt to take control of his thinking and valuing to make more power-enhancing forms does not represent a significant alternative to the reigning technological thinking but rather a more complete version of it. Thus he perpetuates what he is trying to overcome. His creating does not represent our taking back control over ourselves, but following instructions we receive that tell us that taking control is what is most valuable.

> Our whole human existence everywhere sees itself challenged ... to devote itself to the planning and calculating of every thing. What speaks in this challenge? Does it stem merely from man's spontaneous whim? Or are we here already concerned with beings themselves, in such a way that they make a claim on us with respect to their aptness to be planned and calculated? ... To the same degree that Being is challenged, man, too, is challenged, that is, forced to secure all beings that are his concern as the substance for his planning and calculating. (Heidegger, 2002a, 34–35)

However, as Hölderlin puts it, "But where danger is, grows/ The saving power also" (Heidegger, 1993a, 340).

The fact that this technological mindset is sent to us foils our attempt to create and control ourselves all the way down and all the way back, our drive to take up our thrownness being itself something we are inescapably thrown into. This attempt to manufacture meaning is what renders any result meaningless, but the same feature can also give us the meaningfulness we were seeking. We just need to think about our thinking differently. "By this conception of the totality of the technological world, we reduce everything down to man .... Caught up in this conception, we confirm our own opinion that technology is of man's making alone. We fail to hear the claim of Being which speaks in the essence of technology" (Heidegger, 2002a, 34). Hearing this claim means hearing it *as* a claim, as something that comes to us and places obligation on us. It means thinking of our technological way of thinking as itself radically incompatible with the technological mindset. Instead of the transcendental explanation that we are the source of our concepts, they come from being, i.e., no-thing that can serve as a wonder-stopping explanation.

Being granted this thinking which we could not fashion for ourselves, being claimed by being for being, gives us our belonging.

> The granting that sends one way or another into revealing is as such the saving power. For the saving power lets man see and enter into the highest dignity of his essence. This dignity lies in keeping watch over the unconcealment – and with it, from the first, the concealment – of all essential unfolding on this earth .... Everything, then, depends upon this: that we ponder this rising and that, recollecting, we watch over it. (Heidegger, 1993a, 337)

Watching over it means watching it, attending to it by giving it attention, almost a mystical form of phenomenology. (3) Being is the manifestation of (1) beings in their (2) ways of being and we are the clearing in which (1) beings become (3) manifest. We are the location where being happens not because it happens by our doing or in our minds, but because it takes place *as* our thinking, for that is how we let beings come into appearance in their rational form.

<u>Thinking Gives Us Groundless Grounds.</u> In Heidegger's early work, anxiety shows us a world stripped of its worldness – emptied of meaningfulness and repellent to interest (from "inter-esse" – in-being). 1929's "What Is Metaphysics?" connects this mood with philosophical inquiry by ending its detailed examination of anxiety with "the basic question of metaphysics which the nothing itself compels: Why are there beings at all, and why not rather nothing?" (Heidegger, 1993a, 110). Anxiety prevents us from putting things in their comprehensible and usable places in our world, leaving beings as just beings. Standing idle outside the activities that usually draw us into the world and through the day, we can only stare in surprised perplexity at their mere existence, the only feature left to them which now, barren of all intelligibility, confronts us as shocking in its absolute contingency. Why are these things here? Why is anything anywhere? This question has basically the same effect that the mood anxiety does: "it discloses these beings in their full but heretofore concealed strangeness as what is radically other – with respect to the nothing" (Heidegger, 1993a, 103).

A later postscript to the essay adds awe to this pair.

> The lucid courage for essential anxiety assures us the enigmatic possibility of experiencing being. For close by essential anxiety as the horror of the abyss dwells awe. Awe cherishes that locality of the human essence within which humans remain at home in that which endures. (Heidegger, 1998b, 234)

The anxiety that strips away significance to confront beings in their bare thereness, the metaphysical question of why anything is there, and the awe that cherishes their thereness, fit together. All three take us out of our normal teleological interactions with particular entities to place us before beings as a whole or beings as such, the beings qua beings that Aristotle says are the object of first philosophy – the discipline that begins in wonder.

Aristotle sees the point of philosophy to get beyond the puzzlement that provokes our questioning so that we "end up in the contrary and (according to the proverb) the better state, the one that people achieve by learning" the answer (Aristotle, 1988, *Metaphysics* 938a 18–20). For Heidegger, however, "philosophical questions are in principle never settled as if some day one could set them aside" (Heidegger, 2014b, 46). Any answer to the basic question of metaphysics – why is there anything at all – would take the form of an explanation as to why there are beings. With this answer in hand, there's no more need to think about it; wonder has given way to knowledge. As questioning's end, answers are the end of questioning – but genuine thinking does not culminate in closure for Heidegger. With regard to the deepest matters, "questioning is not a mere *prelude* for the sake of presenting something unquestionable as something that had been attained. Questioning is here the beginning and the end" (Heidegger, 2012b, 274/§222). While knowledge is necessary for daily life and appropriate to most disciplines, conclusions bring about the conclusion of philosophizing.

Just as there is an autopilot mode for our average everyday lives of grocery shopping and driving cars which *Being and Time* addressed as a form of inauthenticity, philosophers can fall into the mode of just wheeling out known-by-heart arguments, the way Husserl describes experienced mathematicians running through basic geometrical proofs in "Origin of Geometry." This shuffling around of familiar concepts leads to a thoughtless thinking, an abstracted theorizing that pays as little attention to its thoughts as an experienced driver does to their car. This smooth solving of problems breaks down when it hits up against unthinkable thoughts that resist easy digestion – insoluble problems and ideas that violate logical rules we take for granted, unanswerable questions and inconceivable answers. Seeking these out will strike you as perverse, almost unintelligible, if you only recognize conclusive answers as a satisfactory end of inquiry, but

Heidegger is trying to draw our attention to something that eludes direct expression and explanation and yet is the object of genuine thinking.

> To think Being ... all that is needed is simple wakefulness in the proximity of any random unobtrusive being, an awakening that all of a sudden sees that the being "is."
>
> The awakening for this "it is" of a being, and above all the remaining awake for the "it is," and the watching over the clearing of beings – that constitutes the essence of essential thinking. The "it is" of beings, Being, shows itself, if it does show itself, in each case only "suddenly" .... To think Being requires in each instance a leap, a leap into the groundless from the habitual ground upon which for us beings always rest .... This genuine thinking occurs "by leaps," for it ignores the bridges and railings and ladders of explanation, which always only derives beings from beings .... The open itself secures the essential abode of man, provided man and only he is that being to whom Being illuminates itself. (Heidegger, 1998a, 149–150)

His philosophizing is not in search of an answer but an attitude, a stance, the awakening of the mind that philosophers have been seeking since Socrates. "If the answer could be given it would consist in a transformation of thinking, not in a propositional statement about a matter at stake" (Heidegger, 1993a, 431).

This leads to an atypical view of knowledge and truth.

> Where beings are not very familiar to man and are scarcely and only roughly known by science, the openedness of beings as a whole can prevail more essentially than it can where the familiar and well-known has become boundless, and nothing is any longer able to withstand the business of knowing, since technical mastery over things bears itself without limit. Precisely in the leveling and planing of this omniscience, this mere knowing, the openedness of beings gets flattened out into the apparent nothingness of what is no longer even a matter of indifference, but rather is simply forgotten. (Heidegger, 1993a, 129)

One reason Heidegger never tires of the question of being is that history has never tired of it because it is inexhaustible, as generation after generation generates new answers and new inquiries. "The guiding question of Western philosophy is, 'What is Being?' To *treat* this question as stated is simply to look for an answer .... Developing the guiding question is something essentially different – it is a more original form of inquiry, one which does not crave an answer" (Heidegger, 1979, vol II, 192).

Heidegger ends the Introduction to *Being and Time* by warning us of "the awkwardness and 'inelegance' of expression" of the book that follows, which is due to the fact that "we lack not only most of the words but, above all, the 'grammar'" to say something about being as opposed to beings (Heidegger, 1962, 63/39). Since then, this warning has become a promise.

> The relationship of thinking, being, and language therefore does not lie over against us. We ourselves are held within it. We can neither overtake it, nor even merely catch up with it, because we ourselves are caught up in this relationship. On this we would like to note that *the elaborateness and awkwardness that our contemplation must go through* do not merely stem from the limitations of our capacities, but instead are *essential*. This gives no right to whine about the wretchedness of the human, but *is instead a cause for jubilation over the plenitude of the riddle that remains preserved for thinking*. (Heidegger, 2012a, 155, all italics added)

Its resistance to articulation is at the same time its reservoir of meanings beyond any single articulation. This open-ended polysemy gives it the ability to continuously stimulate and provoke us to think anew if we think about this feature in a new way. The fact that we are always already caught up in it is not the lamentable state of our heteronomy, but our belonging, closeness, intimacy with what we think – we just think ourselves alienated. If we look at our inability to once and for all come to conclusive conclusions that settle the matter from the other side, we can see it as the literally inconceivable generosity of reality in giving us such a bounty of food for thought at this ongoing feast.

Heidegger does give a kind of answer in the form of various epochs' understandings of being, but his goal is different from what we usually expect. For one thing, he draws on the alienness of these ways of thinking to help disrupt the inconspicuousness of our own taken-for-granted one: "What did we seek from this 'historical reflection'? To obtain a distance from what we take as self-evident, from what lies all too close to us" (Heidegger, 2013, 6). This distancing from the conviction in the absolute truth of any one view is one thing this method shares with Husserl's method of bracketing, despite their many deep differences, one reason for the etymological resonance of Heidegger's "epoch" with Husserl's "*epoché*." Other ways of understanding show us that our way of thinking is just one way rather than the way. "Whenever and however we attempt to contemplate thinking, every time a blunt consideration is already revealed to us: there is no thinking as such [*das Denken*]. Thinking – and the talk can be of this alone – is the hidden and innermost dispute of our history. Thinking is what is historical of this history and thus is historical in itself" (Heidegger, 2012a, 93).

Another and more important reason Heidegger spends so much time on these epochal metaphysics is that, as the missives of being, they are the vessel of what can be sacred after the death of God. These (2) ways of being are the issuances of being but, as what enables beings to appear, they are also in a way (3) being itself. This seems contradictory only for what I call an onticology, i.e., an ontology that only recognizes beings and so only has concepts, words, and logical rules appropriate to beings. A more appropriate ontology could accommodate the sameness in difference of the sendings and their sending. "What it gives us to think about, the gift it gives to us, is nothing less than itself – itself which calls on us to enter thought . . . . It entrusts thought to us as our essential destiny, and thus first joins and appropriates us to thought" (Heidegger, 1968, 121). In this light, even the technological attitude that Heidegger presents in such a negative light "is an ordaining of destining, as is every way of revealing" (Heidegger, 1993a, 330).

A kind of dialectic forms between (2) the sendings and (3) their sending (and (1) the sent) where instead of each covering over the other, they can bring each other into the light – or rather, both at the same time. We avoid understanding the sendings as effects of an entity such as ourselves or God when we understand the sender to be nothing beyond or behind the sending itself.

> The leaping-off realm that we have in mind here is, according to the usual way of representing it, the history of Western thinking. In this thinking, beings, as manifoldly experienced in multifariously changing concepts and names, are constantly and at every turn questioned with respect to their [2] being. In the history of this thinking and for it, being comes to shine forth in a certain manner, namely as [2] the being of beings. This shining forth gives a clue about [3] being as such. The clue yields a bit of information about being, according to which being is never first posited by human cognition [transcendental philosophy]. [3] Being proffers itself to humans in that it clearly furnishes to beings as such [2] a temporal play-space. As such a *Geschick*, being essentially comes to be as a self-revealing that at the same time lasts as self-concealing. The history of Western thinking is based in the *Geschick* of being. (Heidegger, 1996a, 75, bracketed comments added)[24]

The "temporal play-space," epochal understanding of being, or historical clearing (basically the same thing) is what metaphysicians spell out – how beings appear to people of that era and culture. Metaphysicians think their epoch's understanding of being by capturing "the totality of beings as such with an eye to their most universal traits" (Heidegger, 1998b, 287). This is what opens up and limits the temporary, temporal space of reason, setting the dimensions within which beings can appear, interact, and be thought and said for that epoch.

Any explanation presupposes an understanding of how the world works, a bounded notion of what counts as a reasonable explanation and what doesn't. A contemporary scientific explanation that appealed to divine intervention to account for observable phenomena would immediately disqualify itself; a medieval account could be disqualified for *not* doing so. Each understanding

---

[24] Here I follow the translators in leaving "*Geschick*" untranslated. It means "sending" with resonances of history and destiny as well.

of being has its own sense of what grounding is and can be, what can be considered a legitimate ground and what can't. We don't think in a vacuum or pure absoluteness but only within a conceptual whole that gives concepts their sense. Since any explanation presupposes a framework that makes that explanation intelligible and plausible, relevant and legitimate, the explanation of *it* would in turn require a larger framework, which would itself need explaining, and so on. There are periodic attempts to bring this to an end with some sort of absolute framework such as god or science or reality, but these are inevitably exposed as presuppositions by later thinkers whose thought does not belong to that way of thinking.

Thus, any attempt to explain the sending of these ways of understanding must employ concepts belonging within one sending or another, e.g., that we think the way we do because of our evolutionary development or because God created our minds in His image. These explanations *of* our understanding take place *within* one or another understanding and so cannot get outside of all of them to say something about them as a whole from a neutral point of view. The only referees we can bring in to call the game play for one of the teams.

Instead of drawing the skeptical conclusion that our thought is all ungrounded and thus illegitimate, we can read the same ideas in the other direction to draw the opposite conclusion. We do have the capacity to explain phenomena in ways that do illuminate and create understanding even though we cannot understand how or why we understand.[25] You can either focus on the fact that we cannot understand our understanding and get seized with cognitive nihilism and despair at the way all our explanations bottom out in groundless abysses, or on the fact that we can and have thought and explained and lived in a world supported by nothing. "At the abyss, thinking finds no more ground. It falls into the bottomless, where nothing bears any longer. But must thinking necessarily be borne? ... Thinking can be borne in that it is suspended."[26] Thinking this both requires and helps bring about a new way of thinking by instituting a new way of thinking of thinking. "This will be an abyss for thinking only of such a sort that

---

[25] I cannot help but think of Hume here, despite Heidegger's rather pointed neglect of him, when he comments on "the whimsical condition of mankind, who must act and reason and believe; though they are not able, by their most diligent enquiry, to satisfy themselves concerning the foundation of these operations, or to remove the objections, which may be raised against them" (Hume, 2007, 117). For an extended discussion of Hume as predecessor to Heidegger (and Wittgenstein), see Braver 2012b.

[26] Heidegger, 2012a, 145. "Being, the never autochthonous, is the groundless. This seems to be a lack, though only if calculated in terms of beings, and it appears as an abyss in which we founder without support in our relentless pursuit of beings. In fact we surely fall into the abyss, we find no ground, as long as we know and seek a ground only in the form of a being and hence never carry out the leap into Being or leave the familiar landscape of the oblivion of Being. This leap requires no digressions or formalities" (Heidegger, 1998a, 150).

thinking as something transformed finds in this abyss a fitting realm for itself" (Heidegger, 2012a, 106). Thinking is by its very nature conditioned by the understanding it belongs to – "we have left behind us the presumption of all unconditionedness" (Heidegger, 2001, 179) – so the unconditioned, absolute thoughts whose lack we mourn is not a genuine possibility.

Heidegger argues that not only *is* there no finally grounded ground, there *could* be none. He reasons his way to the underside of reason.

> Being 'is' in essence: ground/reason.[27] Therefore being can never first have a ground/reason which would supposedly ground it. Accordingly, ground/reason is missing from being. Ground/reason remains at a remove from being. Being 'is' the abyss [*Abgrund*] in the sense of such a remaining-apart of reason from being. To the extent that being as such grounds, it remains groundless. (Heidegger, 1996a, 51)

In fact, it is only groundless grounds that can ground us just as only heteronomy can give us ethical obligations and no-thing yield things. The ground of reason must be arational because it cannot supply the kind of grounding that reason itself requires. What we make of this, however, depends on how we think of thinking.

> Insofar as being essentially comes to be as ground/reason, it has no ground/reason. However this is not because it founds itself, but because every foundation – even and especially self-founded ones – remain inappropriate to being as ground/reason .... Being *qua* being remains ground-less .... If we think about this, and if we persist in such thinking, then we notice that we have leaped off from the realm of previous thinking and are in the leap. But do we not fall into the fathomless with this leap? Yes and no. Yes – insofar as being can no longer be given a basis in the sense of beings and explained in terms of beings. No – insofar as being is now finally to be thought *qua* being. As what is to be thought, it becomes, from out of its truth, what gives a measure. The manner in which thinking thinks must conform to this measure. But it is not possible for us to seize upon this measure and what it offers through a computing and gauging. For us it remains that which is immeasurable. However, so little does the leap allow thinking to fall into the fathomless in the sense of the complete void that in fact it first allows thinking to respond to being *qua* being, that is, to the truth of being. (Heidegger, 1996a, 111)

Our understanding of being gives us the units of measurement for reasoning, so to speak; we do not have to take measures to create it, a creation which would have to be done without rational criteria *ex hypothesi*.

None of the sent concepts can apply to the sending itself and these are all we have. A quest for absolute rationality views this as a loss, but the curtailing of explanation leads to the open-ended questioning of wonder.

---

[27] "Ground/reason" is the translator's way of rendering "*Grund*," which means both.

> Wonder displaces man into and before beings as such.... This displacement is beyond explanation, for all explanation here necessarily falls short and comes too late, since it could only move within, and would have to appeal to, something that was first encountered as unconcealed in the displacement that casts asunder. All explanation is directed to some being, already unconcealed, from which alone an explanatory cause can drawn. (Heidegger, 1994a, 147)

Each theory attempts to bring inquiry to a conclusion, but looking at them from the perspective of history's incommensurable multiplicity shows each one as perpetuating the seeking – in its very attempt to draw the process to a close. Hegel found this to be the lesson history teaches us when we see every thinker shaking their head at how unwittingly misguided all previous thinkers have been, yet utterly convinced that this unceasing pattern will not fall upon them.

The broad overview of history shows us what no conviction in the final truth of any single view can see – the generous fertility of reality that generates so many different ways of thinking about it.[28]

> No wonder then that we no longer notice at all the unheard-of sense of this sentence "being is," much less are touched by it to the point where our entire nature is so shaken that it will never again be the same. Through the centuries this sentence, in many vagrant variations and in many ways has, explicitly or tacitly, been and remained the leading theme of thinking.... And yet the day may come when someone will find the sentence astonishing nonetheless, and will notice that all the centuries that have passed away have not been able to diminish it – that unbeknownst to us it has remained as problematical as ever. (Heidegger, 1968, 179–180)

Aristotle nailed it early on – being *is* said in many ways, he just could not have foreseen that it could and would be said in innumerably many more. Grasping and celebrating that rich fecundity is what brings Heidegger to embrace aporias instead of seeking for them to be solved, to maintain questioning as an attitude rather than a preliminary phase to be resolved.

Dwelling and meditating on this marvel can restore to us some of the meaningfulness that religion gave the medievals – it can fill us with awe, give us direction and purpose, make life significant and worth living. It can battle nihilism not by shining the light of reason on everything, but by protecting the darkness.

> The provenance of the basic principles of thinking, the place of the thinking that posits these propositions, the essence of the place named here and of its location, all of this remains veiled in the dark for us. This darkness is perhaps

---

[28] This may explain the limitation Heidegger often places on the Greeks' insights, otherwise so deep: as the beginners, they did not have access to the insights that a history of diverse views can give.

> in play for all thinking at all times. Humans cannot set it aside. Rather they must learn to acknowledge the dark as something unavoidable and to keep at bay those prejudices that would destroy the lofty reign of the dark. Thus the dark remains distinct from the pitch-black as the mere and utter absence of light. The dark, however, is the secret of the light. (Heidegger, 2012a, 88)

Philosophy's faith in the universal reach of reason makes it encompass all within our measure. This does not expand us out to the cosmos but shrinks the universe down to the size and shape of our thoughts and desires, leading to a diminished sense of who we are and what there is. But "releasement toward things and openness to the mystery . . . grant us the possibility of dwelling in the world in a totally different way" (Heidegger, 1966, 55).

This is the ethical side of epochal destiny of thinking, providing us with a way of dwelling, of being at home on this earth we were thrown into, of living in families and communities, of celebrating festivals and commemorating death. This overcomes nihilism and "gives back to things, to beings, their weight (Being)" (Heidegger, 2014b, 12). We make a home of this earth by embracing the traditions we find ourselves within, not by trying to create ourselves ex nihilo or choosing only what satisfies our drives. Our thrownness into an understanding of being eliminates both the possibility of absolute justification and at the same time, any need for such reassurance. The fact that from the perspective of the history of being no particular understanding can claim absolute truth does not make them equal to *us*. We are thrown into our particular understanding which gives it greater influence on our thinking than the dead options of earlier periods. A deep appreciation of thrownness takes both absolute foundationalism and relativism off the table at a stroke, for these epochal understandings of being, temporary as they may be, do in fact organize our thinking authoritatively. This is how we think.

Conclusion: Thinking in Question

> What is called thinking? We must guard against the blind urge to snatch at a quick answer in the form of a formula. We must stay with the question.
> Heidegger, *What Is Called Thinking?*, 48

Thinking Is Changing. Ever since Socrates challenged his fellow Athenians to think for themselves, philosophers have sought intellectual independence by using thought to separate themselves from anything that could impinge on their autonomy – society, tradition, the body, senses, emotions. The attempt to understand the world has not been, or has not only been, a sober seeking of disinterested knowledge but a drive toward control and power. Heidegger argues that science is a form of technology rather than the other way around;

where technological devices make over the world to make it more conducive to our actions, he sees science as a kind of intellectual tool for making reality conform to our ways of understanding. The practical mastery over nature that technology gives us is a secondary echo of this initiating a priori reduction of the real to the rational. Whatever doesn't fit our preconceived demands gets dismissed as unreal, merely subjective.[29]

> Today a world dominates in which the decisive question runs: How do I have to represent nature in the sequence of its appearances to myself, so that I am in a position to make secure predictions about all and everything? The answer to this question is that it is compulsory to represent nature as a totality of energy particles of existing mass, the reciprocal movements of which are to be mathematically calculable. Descartes already says to the piece of wax that he holds before his eyes: "You are nothing other than an extended, flexible, and mutable thing," and thus I proclaim myself to know everything about you that there is to know of you. (Heidegger, 2003, 8)

We inflate our knowledge by shrinking that which we seek to know down to those features that are knowable by us. Thus, "modern man, Cartesian man, *se solum alloquendo*, only talks to himself" because "the object is constituted by representation. The representation, namely, that is prior in regards to the object, posits the object across from it, in such a way that the object is never able to first presence from itself" (Heidegger, 2003, 37, 72).

This is how Kant's transcendental philosophy guarantees science, purchasing the total knowability of everything at the price of giving up anything that could ever be beyond us.[30] The epistemological quest to understand all there is rests on the anthropocentric equation that identifies making sense with making sense to us, acknowledging in principle only the standards we design to recognize as "man fights for the position in which he can be that being who gives to every being the measure and draws up the guidelines" (Heidegger, 2002b, 71). Thinking then becomes a Procrustean bed that cuts off whatever does not fit contemporary notions of thinkability. Unthinkable aporias can be nothing more than temporary problems to be dissolved by their solutions.

Ironically, the effect of this attempted absorption of reality is to alienate us from the world as it becomes an object and ourselves as mortals born to the earth who become subjects, as our attempt to get what we want drives away that which we want most. You cannot have a belonging with that which belongs to you; giving birth to yourself may create a tremendous sense of power, but it also

---

[29] "If one is oriented primarily by Thinghood, these latter qualities [like beautiful or useful] must be taken as non-quantifiable value-predicates by which what is in the first instance just a material Thing, gets stamped" (Heidegger, 1962, 132/99, bracketed comment added).
[30] On this, see Braver 2012a, 2013a, 2015a, 2017, 2020, 2024a.

takes away the possibility of having a family. The view of rationality that has been common in philosophy, Heidegger concludes, bears the seeds of nihilism within itself.

> The unique unleashing of the demand to render reasons threatens everything of humans' being-at-home and robs them of the roots of their subsistence, the roots from out of which every great human age, every world-opening spirit, every molding of the human form has thus far grown . . . . The claim of the mighty Principle of rendering reasons [i.e., the Principle of Reason that everything has a reason and thus can and must be rationally judged] withdraws the subsistence from contemporary humanity. We could also say that the more decisively humans try to harness the "mega-energies" that would, once and for all, satisfy all human energy needs, the more impoverished becomes the human faculty for building and dwelling in the realm of what is essential. There is an enigmatic interconnection between the demand to render reasons and the withdrawal of roots. (Heidegger, 1996a, 30–31, bracketed comment added)

Protecting mystery as mystery by not demanding that it account for itself before the tribunal of our reason, on the other hand, keeps open the space for what exceeds the grasp of our intellect. There must be something before and underneath us if we are to stand and take sustenance: "I know that, according to our human experience and history, everything essential and great has arisen solely out of the fact that humans had a home and were rooted in a tradition" (Heidegger, 2009b, 325). So many centuries later, we must recollect Socrates' epistemic humility that maintains that the only knowledge we can have is that we cannot have any knowledge – nothing final, nothing absolute, nothing that conclusively closes off and closes down further questioning.

Thinking historically about the historical thinking of being changes the way we look at it. We come to see it not as a series of eternal statements trying to settle issues definitively, each one ending in despair as it gets put aside in favor of a new timeless theory. Instead, it looks like philosophers coming together to discuss the many ways that being speaks to them, collectively collaborating in a sempiternal dialogue on how being variously appears throughout time. The Western tradition as a whole becomes a Socratic, aporetic, open-ended dialogue where we help each other to a wisdom that cannot be separated from profound ignorance rather than a Platonic monologue-with-pliable-audience whose purpose is to ascend the crowd of squabbling *doxa* to the one true transcendent *episteme*. The latter is an attempt to escape death in a realm of timeless thought, whereas the former is a cheerful acceptance of our mortality, of the temporality and hence temporariness of all of our views.

Heidegger accepted this mortal wisdom for himself, dramatically altering his own writing and thought when that which is thought speaks differently to him. "When thinking is addressed by an issue and then goes after this, it can happen that it changes along the way. Thus it is advisable in what follows to attend more to the *path* and less to the content" (Heidegger, 2012a, 108). We must attend to the path not because it is more important than the content but because it *is* the content of thinking, hence the epigraph of his collected writings: ways, not works. What matters are not works or Truth, but working toward truths, thinking about being as it unconceals itself to us. Unlike the subject determining the measure, "as what is to be thought, [being qua being] becomes, from out of its truth, what gives a measure. The manner in which thinking thinks must conform to this measure" (Heidegger, 1996a, 111). We co-respond to these revealings in whatever way seems best at the time, not by fixing a vocabulary or set of concepts in place but by listening and responding to that experience, that reading of a text. "For the author himself, however, there remains the quandary of always having to speak in the language most opportune for each of the various stations on his way" (Heidegger, 1993a, 211–212). Heidegger continually tried to say being and he continually said it differently, as did the tradition, just as Cézanne repeatedly painted the same mountain and yet never painted the same mountain twice.

As we have seen, Heidegger repeatedly read his own earlier works in new ways when he went back to them. This is also how he read the canon, as he says in a very late interview that traditional philosophy

> has come to an end, but it has not become null and void for us; rather, it has become newly present through dialogue. My entire work in lectures and exercises in the past thirty years was mainly just an interpretation of Western philosophy. The return to the historical foundations of thought, the thinking-through of the questions that have remained unasked since the time of Greek philosophy, that is no severance from the tradition. (Heidegger, 2009b, 328)

His work consists in a dialogue with the tradition, both because that is what he thinks from and because that is what he is trying to think away from. "Our own way derives from such thinking. It therefore remains necessarily bound to a dialogue with traditional thinking. And since our way is concerned with thinking for the specific purpose of learning it, the dialogue must discuss the nature of traditional thinking" (Heidegger, 1968, 55). Yet this attempt to get away must itself be thought anew or else it does not actually get away from it; even a contradiction or denial of the tradition just collapses into an extension of the same way of thinking since contradictions form part of standard logic. His dialogical way of reading these works does something different from merely repeating them faithfully or imposing his own views on them; it renders them "newly present." This escapes the binary options standard logic offers, offering Heidegger a new way to be new, a different way to differ from the past that neither simply continues nor rebels against it.

Heidegger finds what exceeds us within the very tradition that seems intent on stamping out anything in principle beyond us, as his reading in this unheard-of way uncovers previously unheard ideas in familiar, canonical texts. They are textually grounded, but the text turns out to be polysemous, capable of saying more than we usually credit.

> The thinkers' language tells what is. To hear it is in no case easy .... To acknowledge and respect consists in letting every thinker's thought come to us as something in each case unique, never to be repeated, inexhaustible – and being shaken to the depths by what is unthought in his thought. What is unthought in a thinker's thought is not a lack inherent in his thought. What is *un*-thought is there in each case only as the un-*thought*. (Heidegger, 1968, 76)

Other thoughts can be found there if we allow ourselves new conceptions of what it means to be there, conceptions that fall outside the confines of the normal present-absent contraries.

He finds in these seemingly well-known works ideas that help him think his own topics, and the very fact that he can find these alternate readings is part of this help. Showing that great texts say more than any reading, even that of their author, can ever exhaust helps loosen the grip of the notion that we the subject are in complete charge of our thought. This is one of the ways

> language speaks, not humans. Humans only speak inasmuch as they respond to language on the basis of the *Geschick* .... Polysemy is always an historical polysemy. It springs from the fact that in the speaking of language we ourselves are at times, according to the *Geschick* of being, struck, that means addressed, differently by the being of beings. (Heidegger, 1996a, 96)[31]

Just as being addresses us differently in different epochs through diverse understandings of being, so are those dictations of being – the great metaphysical texts – always read anew.

> It would be silly to say the medieval theologians misunderstood Aristotle; rather, they understood him differently, responding to the different manner in which being proffered itself to them. Then again, the *Geschick* of being is different for Kant. A different understanding becomes a misunderstanding only where it comes to a peak in a uniquely possible truth and simultaneously is subsumed under the order of what is to be understood. (Heidegger, 1996a, 79)

---

[31] On polysemy, see Braver 2022, 2023a.

The metaphysicians each heard being speaking to them in a different way, and each read the way previous metaphysicians had heard being in a different way. This is how a dialogue with the tradition can render it "newly present" – new ideas within it are present in a new way. This is especially important since these understandings of being are not writings *about* being so much as writings *of* being. They are the way that being manifests itself to thought, so acknowledging that there is more to being than we can know or circumscribe means, on the one hand, that we cannot predict what new epochs will bring in the future, but it also means that we cannot exhaustively determine what any epochal being was in the past. Indeed, this very way of reading shakes up the traditional temporal tenses, a long-time project of Heidegger's.

> People still hold the view that what is handed down to us by tradition is what in reality lies behind us – while in fact it comes toward us because we are its captives and destined to it. The purely historical view of tradition and the course of history is one of those vast self-deceptions in which we must remain entangled as long as we are still not really thinking. That self-deception about history prevents us from hearing the language of the thinkers. We do not hear it rightly, because we take that language to be mere expression, setting forth philosophers' views. (Heidegger, 1968, 76)

A dialogue with the tradition renders it newly present by bringing it to us within a new kind of present, one that integrates past and future rather than excluding them.

Despite Plato's stated attempts to surpass *doxa* to reach *episteme* within his dialogues, we can find a different model of thinking in the dialogue form of his writings itself. Attending to this, we should not fixate on any results or propositions. After all, "if we take up one of Plato's dialogues, and scrutinize and judge its 'content' ... not a single one of Plato's dialogues arrives at a palpable, unequivocal result which sound common sense could, as the saying goes, hold on to" (ibid., 71). No, the ultimate lesson we learn from Plato's dialogues is how to think as an ongoing, open-ended dialogue, for this is how his works actually occurred in history – generating new readings and interpretations generation after generation.

> There is no universal schema which could be applied mechanically to the interpretation of the writings of thinkers, or even to a single work of a single thinker. A dialogue of Plato – the *Phaedrus*, for example, the conversation on Beauty – can be interpreted in totally different spheres and respects, according to totally different implications and problematics. This multiplicity of possible interpretations does not discredit the strictness of the thought content. For all true thought remains open to more than one interpretation – and this by reason of its nature .... Multiplicity of meanings is the element in which all thought must move in order to be strict thought. (ibid.)

We can briefly read this rereadability in Kant. Kant deserves a primary place in the history of being proposed for Part Two of *Being and Time* because he was "the first and only person who has gone any stretch of the way towards investigating the dimension of Temporality," in particular in regards to "the question whether and to what extent the Interpretation of Being and the phenomenon of time have been brought together thematically in the course of the history of ontology" (Heidegger, 1962, 45/23). He is also, uncoincidentally in my view, the philosopher who introduced the hermeneutic right to read new ideas in old texts even if those ideas conflict with the text's surface sense. This is because we can understand an author "even better than he understood himself" since the author "sometimes spoke, or even thought, contrary to his own intention" (Kant, 1999, A314/B370).[32] In other words, we can find their unsaid within what they said. Kant can be read as both creating the modern, subject-centered thinking where, as Deleuze sums up his thought, "the first thing that the Copernican Revolution teaches us is that it is we who are giving the orders" (Deleuze, 1984, 14), and at the same time as offering us ways to think that can help us escape it.

The first *Critique* opens on the inescapable way that "reason falls into this perplexity" by being "burdened with questions which it cannot dismiss ... but which it also cannot answer, since they transcend every capacity of human reason" (Kant, 1999, Avii). The destiny of our thought is to think what it cannot genuinely, fully think and certainly cannot know; even the success of Kant's critical project cannot dispel the violating ideas it warns us against. We are fated, as Heidegger also says, to think in an abyss that we cannot bear but which may bear us. "The unconditioned necessity, which we need so indispensably as the ultimate sustainer of all things, is for human reason the true abyss .... One cannot resist the thought of it, but one also cannot bear it" (ibid., A613/B641, see also A296/B353–A298/B355). When he introduced these transcendent Ideas into his discussion, he found himself without an appropriate vocabulary, like Heidegger in the Introduction to *Being and Time*, and looked to the tradition for help in saying and thinking what he wanted since we do not have the power to dictate to language. He uses ideas he finds in the canon – here, Plato's Ideas – differently than their author did – a violent interpretation.[33]

---

[32] On this rereading of Kant, see Braver 2021, 2023b. The reading given here of Kant is mine, not Heidegger's, but it uses what I take to be a Heideggerian hermeneutical approach.

[33] "In the great wealth of our languages, the thinking mind nevertheless often finds itself at a loss for an expression that exactly suits its concept, and lacking this it is able to make itself rightly intelligible neither to others nor even to itself. Coining new words is a presumption to legislate in language that rarely succeeds, and before we have recourse to this dubious means it is advisable to look around in a dead and learned language to see if an expression occurs in it that is suitable to

He reaches the same conclusion in his moral philosophy, as the *Grounding* ends when it locates "the extreme limit of all moral inquiry." We cannot claim knowledge of the intelligible self from whom we get our moral law, nor how we can, nor why we do, follow the law. The only way to make such matters intelligible would be to bring them within the phenomenal realm of causal explanation which would eliminate the very qualities of free morality we seek to explain. Nor, however, can we simply pass the matter over in silence as a sheer unintelligible mystery. Instead, the moral that the final lines of the book leave us with is that we must think its unthinkability. "And so even though we do not indeed grasp the practical unconditioned necessity of the moral imperative, we do nevertheless grasp its inconceivability. This is all that can be fairly asked of a philosophy which strives in its principles to reach the very limit of human reason" (Kant, 2010, 61–62). Rather than resting with a conclusive answer, the inconceivable is what drives us to continue thinking. "The satisfaction of reason is only further and further postponed by the continual inquiry after the condition. Reason, therefore, restlessly seeks the unconditionally necessary and sees itself compelled to assume this without having any means of making such necessity conceivable" (ibid., 62). The great thinker of the Enlightenment is at the same time a deep diver of inconceivable, unending abysses. We can read this other side of him because there only exist the various phenomenal readings which are true by unconcealing previously unseen meanings rather than by corresponding to some one unwaveringly unambiguous interpretation held within a "Kant in himself" (Heidegger, 1997b, 175).

While such a "violent Heideggerian interpretation" is often seen as an arrogant imposition of his own thoughts onto the thinkers he reads, he describes it as "an attempt to question what has not been said, instead of writing in a fixed way about what Kant said" (ibid.). His readings resemble Nietzsche's philosophizing with a hammer (the subtitle of *Twilight of the Idols*) which, instead of smashing things apart, is a tapping with a tuning fork. Where Nietzsche was listening for hollowness, Heidegger opens himself up to faint echoes resonating beneath the louder, more obvious interpretations. This sensitive attentiveness is how phenomenology philosophizes, how poets write, and ultimately how *all* careful thought thinks – by responding – but we can either go with our

---

this concept; and even if the ancient use of this expression has become somewhat unsteady owing to the inattentiveness of its authors, it is better to fix on the meaning that is proper to it (even if it is doubtful whether it always had exactly this sense) than to ruin our enterprise by making ourselves unintelligible" (Kant, 1999, A312/B568-9). Kant acknowledges that Plato's Idea goes counter to his own in many ways but "the lofty language that served him in this field is surely quite susceptible of a milder interpretation, and one that accords better with the nature of things" (ibid., A314/B371 note). Kant does not hesitate to adapt Plato's terms and Ideas to his own project.

immediate surface response or keep listening for what else can be heard. Studying history helps us be patiently open to alternatives by displaying the variety of readings that great works have given rise to.

Since there is always more to learn, true thinkers are not those who have arrived at finished views in need of no revision but rather those who know how to perpetually learn. "The teacher must be capable of being more teachable than the apprentices. The teacher is far less assured of his ground than those who learn are of theirs" (Heidegger, 1968, 15). This openness, this listening, this perpetual openness to learning is the one true lesson that is always taught no matter what the subject matter since all teaching must to some degree teach the student how to learn the lesson. "The real teacher, in fact, lets nothing else be learned than – learning" (ibid.). This is particularly relevant in learning our topic, thinking, since thinking is nothing other than this. "We are here attempting to learn thinking . . . . To learn means to make everything we do answer to whatever essentials address themselves to us at a given time. Depending on the kind of essentials, depending on the realm from which they address us, the answer and with it the kind of learning differs" (ibid., 14). This is a lesson we can learn from Kant – from a certain rereading of Kant. Heidegger defines Kant's greatest lesson as "precisely a question of becoming certain of this finitude in order to hold oneself in it" (Heidegger, 1997b, 152). Despite his assurances that he has definitively determined all transcendental faculties once and for all, Kant also teaches us that we are thrown into the very structures of thinking and acting that enable us to be spontaneous, that we can neither act on the ultimate source of our actions nor know the fundamental reasons of our knowledge. He builds his foundation on an abyss which we stare into every time we think – an abyss that "stares back into you," as Nietzsche puts it (Nietzsche, 2001a, 146), but from which most of us avert our gaze. Plato's dialogues taught us to be open to what we hear. Aristotle's analysis of crafts showed us how to be attentive to the particularities of each situation and that you learn these by repeatedly doing them, a kind of learning and knowing that is intrinsically bound up with time. This last point is especially salient for us as "we are trying to learn thinking . . . . It is a craft" (Heidegger, 1968, 16).

Bibliography

Aristotle (1988) *A New Aristotle Reader*. Princeton University Press.

Aristotle (2019) *Nicomachean Ethics*. Third edition. Translated by T. Irwin. Hackett Publishing.

Blattner, W. D. (1999) *Heidegger's Temporal Idealism*. Cambridge University Press.

Braver, L. (2007) *A Thing of This World: A History of Continental Anti-realism*. Northwestern University Press.

Braver, L. (2012a) "A Brief History of Continental Realism." *Continental Philosophy Review*, 45(2), 261–289. doi: https://doi.org/10.1007/s11007-012-9220-2.

Braver, L. (2012b) *Groundless Grounds: A Study of Wittgenstein and Heidegger*. Massachusetts Institute of Technology Press.

Braver, L. (2013a) "On Not Settling the Question of Realism." In Michael Austin, Paul J. Ennis, Fabio Gironi, Thomas Gokey, and Robert Jackson, eds., *Speculations IV: Speculative Realism*, pp. 9–14. Punctum Books.

Braver, L. (2013b) "Never Mind: Thinking of Subjectivity in the Dreyfus-McDowell Debate." In J. K. Schear, ed., *Mind, Reason, and Being-in-the-World: The McDowell-Dreyfus Debate*. Routledge, pp. 143–62.

Braver, L. (2014) *Heidegger: Thinking of Being*. Polity Press (Key Contemporary Thinkers).

Braver, L. (2015a) "Thoughts on the Unthinkable." *Parrhesia: A Journal of Critical Philosophy*, 24 (December), pp. 1–16.

Braver, L. (2015b) *Division III of Heidegger's Being and Time: The Unanswered Question of Being*. Massachusetts Institute of Technology Press.

Braver, L. (2017) "Before Infinitude: A Levinasian Response to Meillassoux's Speculative Realism." In Marie-Eve Morin, ed., *Continental Realism and Its Discontents*, pp. 59–80. Edinburgh University Press.

Braver, L. (2020) "The Real Scandal." In Gregor Kroupa and Jure Simoniti, eds., *New Realism and Contemporary Philosophy*, pp. 85–98. Bloomsbury.

Braver, L. (2021) "Introduction: Why (Heidegger) Scholarship Is Generational." *Gatherings: The Heidegger Circle Annual*, 11, pp. 1–19.

Braver, L. (2022) "How to Say the Same Thing: Heidegger's Vocabulary and Grammar of Being." *Review of Metaphysics*, 75(3), pp. 525–559.

Braver, L. (2023a) "Eternal Return Hermeneutics in Nietzsche, Heidegger, and Derrida." *Open Philosophy*, 6(1). doi: https://doi.org/10.1515/opphil-2022-0267.

Braver, L. (2023b) "Derrida's *Donner – le temps* Session 6: What This Previously Unpublished Session Teaches Us about *Given Time: I*." *Open Philosophy*, 6(1), pp. 20220271. https://doi.org/10.1515/opphil-2022-0271.

Braver, L. (2024a) "What Does the Spoon Taste? Heideggerian Epistemology and Speculative Realism." In Charles Johns and Hilan Bensusan, eds., *Speculative Realism Today*. Bloomsbury.

Braver, L. (2024b) "Nothing Matters: Heidegger on Nietzsche on Nihilism." In Kevin Aho, Megan Altman, and Hans Pedersen, eds., *The Routledge Handbook of Contemporary Existentialism*. Routledge, pp. 302–14.

Brooks, R. A. (1991) "Intelligence without Representation," *Artificial Intelligence*, 47(1), pp. 139–159.

Carman, T. (2007) *Heidegger's Analytic: Interpretation, Discourse and Authenticity in Being and Time*. Cambridge University Press.

Clark, A. (1998) *Being There: Putting Brain, Body, and World Together Again*. Massachusetts Institute of Technology Press.

Cottingham, J., Stoothoff, R., and Murdoch, D., eds. (2013) *The Philosophical Writings of Descartes: Volume 1*. Cambridge University Press.

Crowell, S. G., and Malpas, J. (2007) *Transcendental Heidegger*. Stanford University Press.

Damasio, A. (2005) *Descartes' Error: Emotion, Reason, and the Human Brain*. Penguin Books.

Deleuze, G. (1984) *Kant's Critical Philosophy*. University of Minnesota Press.

Dreyfus, H. L. (1986) *Mind over Machine: The Power of Human Intuition and Expertise in the Era of the Computer*. Free Press.

Dreyfus, H. L. (1991) *Being-in-the-World: A Commentary on Heidegger's Being and Time, Division I*. Massachusetts Institute of Technology Press.

Dreyfus, H. L. (1992) *What Computers Still Can't Do: A Critique of Artificial Reason*. Massachusetts Institute of Technology Press.

Dreyfus, H. L. (1996) "The Current Relevance of Merleau-Ponty's Phenomenology of Embodiment," *The Electronic Journal of Analytic Philosophy*, 4(4), pp. 1–16.

Dreyfus, H. L. (1999) "The Primacy of Phenomenology over Logical Analysis," *Philosophical Topics*, 27(2), pp. 3–24.

Dreyfus, H. L. (2000) "Merleau-Ponty's Critique of Husserl's (and Searle's) Concept of Intentionality." In Dorothea Olkowski and Lawrence Hass, eds., *Rereading Merleau-Ponty: Essays beyond the Continental-Analytic Divide*, pp. 33–52. Humanity Books.

Dreyfus, H. L. (2004) "Could Anything be More Intelligible Than Everyday Intelligibility? Reinterpreting Division I of *Being and Time* in the Light of Division II." *Bulletin of Science Technology & Society*, 24(3), pp. 265–274.

Dreyfus, H. L. (2005) "Overcoming the Myth of the Mental: How Philosophers Can Profit from the Phenomenology of Everyday Expertise," *Proceedings and Addresses of the American Philosophical Association*, 79(2), pp. 47–65.

Dreyfus, H. L. (2007a) "Response to McDowell," *Inquiry*, 50(4), pp. 371–377.

Dreyfus, H. L. (2007b) "The Return of the Myth of the Mental," *Inquiry*, 50(4), pp. 352–365.

Guignon, C. B. (1983) *Heidegger and the Problem of Knowledge*. Hackett Publishing.

Haugeland, J. (1985) *Artificial Intelligence: The Very Idea*. Massachusetts Institute of Technology Press.

Haugeland, J. (1998) *Having Thought: Essays in the Metaphysics of Mind*. Harvard University Press.

Heidegger, M. (1962) *Being and Time*. Harper & Row.

Heidegger, M. (1966) *Discourse on Thinking*. Harper & Row.

Heidegger, M. (1968) *What Is Called Thinking?* First edition. Harper & Row (Religious Perspectives, vol. 21).

Heidegger, M. (1972) *On Time and Being*. Harper & Row.

Heidegger, M. (1977) *The Question Concerning Technology, and Other Essays*. First edition. Translated by W. Lovitt. Harper & Row (Harper Colophon Books).

Heidegger, M. (1979) *Nietzsche*. First edition. Harper & Row.

Heidegger, M. (1984a) *Early Greek Thinking*. Harper & Row.

Heidegger, M. (1984b) *The Metaphysical Foundations of Logic*. Indiana University Press.

Heidegger, M. (1985) *History of the Concept of Time: Prolegomena*. Indiana University Press (Studies in Phenomenology and Existential Philosophy).

Heidegger, M. (1988) *The Basic Problems of Phenomenology*. Second edition. Indiana University Press (Studies in Phenomenology and Existential Philosophy).

Heidegger, M. (1993) *Basic Writings: from Being and Time (1927) to The Task of Thinking (1964)*. Revised and expanded edition. HarperSanFrancisco.

Heidegger, M. (1994) *Basic Questions of Philosophy Selected "Problems" of "Logic."* Indiana University Press.

Heidegger, M. (1996a) *The Principle of Reason*. Indiana University Press.

Heidegger, M. (1996b) *Hölderlin's Hymn "The Ister."* Indiana University Press.

Heidegger, M. (1997a) *Phenomenological Interpretation of Kant's Critique of Pure Reason*. Indiana University Press.

Heidegger, M. (1997b). *Kant and the Problem of Metaphysics, Fifth Edition, Enlarged*. Indiana University Press. doi: https://doi.org/10.2307/j.ctvswx7ww.

Heidegger, M. (1998a) *Parmenides*. Indiana University Press.

Heidegger, M. (1998b) *Pathmarks*. Cambridge University Press.

Heidegger, M. (2001) *Poetry, Language, Thought*. Perennial Classics.

Heidegger, M. (2002a) *Identity and Difference*. University of Chicago Press.

Heidegger, M. (2002b) *Off the Beaten Track*. Cambridge University Press.

Heidegger, M. (2003) *Four Seminars*. Indiana University Press (Studies in Continental Thought).

Heidegger, M. (2005) *Introduction to Phenomenological Research*. Indiana University Press.

Heidegger, M. (2009a) *Basic Concepts of Aristotelian Philosophy*. Indiana University Press (Studies in Continental Thought).

Heidegger, M. (2009b) *The Heidegger Reader*. Indiana University Press (Studies in Continental Thought).

Heidegger, M. (2012a) *Bremen and Freiburg Lectures Insight into That Which Is and Basic Principles of Thinking*. Bloomington: Indiana University Press (Studies in Continental Thought).

Heidegger, M. (2012b) *Contributions to Philosophy (of the Event)*. Indiana University Press (Studies in Continental Thought).

Heidegger, M. (2013) *The Essence of Truth: On Plato's Cave Allegory and Theaetetus*. Bloomsbury Academic.

Heidegger, M. (2014a) *Hölderlin's Hymns "Germania" and "The Rhine."* Indiana University Press (Studies in Continental Thought).

Heidegger, M. (2014b) *Introduction to Metaphysics*. Second edition. Yale University Press.

Heidegger, M. (2015) *The Beginning of Western Philosophy: Interpretation of Anaximander and Parmenides*. Indiana University Press.

Heidegger, M. (2018) *Hölderlin's Hymn "Remembrance."* Indiana University Press (Studies in Continental Thought).

Heidegger, M., McNeill, W., and Walker, N. (1995) *The Fundamental Concepts of Metaphysics: World, Finitude, Solitude*. Indiana University Press.

Hume, D., and Steinberg, E. (1993) *An Enquiry Concerning Human Understanding; [with] A Letter from a Gentleman to His Friend in Edinburgh; [and] An Abstract of a Treatise of Human Nature*. Hackett Publishing.

Kant, I. (1999). *Critique of Pure Reason*. Edited by Paul Guyer and Allen W. Wood. . Cambridge: Cambridge University Press.

Kant, I. (2010) *Grounding for the Metaphysics of Morals on a Supposed Right to Lie Because of Philanthropic Concerns*. Third ed. Indianapolis: Hackett Publishing (Hackett Classics Series).

Kiverstein, J., and Wheeler, M. (2012) *Heidegger and Cognitive Science*. Palgrave Macmillan (New Directions in Philosophy and Cognitive Science).

Nietzsche, F. (1968) *The Will to Power*. Knopf Doubleday Publishing Group.

Nietzsche, F. (2001b) *The Gay Science*, ed. Bernard Williams, trans. Josefine Nauckhoff. Cambridge University Press.

Nietzsche, F. (2006) *Nietzsche: Thus Spoke Zarathustra*. First Edition. Edited by R. Pippin. Translated by A.D. Caro. Cambridge University Press.

Nietzsche, F., and Norman, J. (2001a) *Beyond Good and Evil: Prelude to a Philosophy of the Future*. Edited by R.-P. Horstmann. Cambridge University Press.

Okrent, M. (1988) *Heidegger's Pragmatism: Understanding, Being, and the Critique of Metaphysics*. Cornell University Press.

Plato (2002) *Plato: Five Dialogues: Euthyphro, Apology, Crito, Meno, Phaedo*. Hackett Publishing.

Richardson, J. (1991) *Existential Epistemology: A Heideggerian Critique of the Cartesian Project*. Clarendon Press.

Rorty, R. (1979) *Philosophy and the Mirror of Nature*. Princeton: University Press.

Rorty, R. (1982) *Consequences of Pragmatism: Essays, 1972–1980*. Minneapolis: University of Minnesota Press.

Rorty, R. (1991) *Essays on Heidegger and Others*. Cambridge: University Press (Philosophical Papers, v. 2).

Winograd, T., and Flores, F. (1986) *Understanding Computers and Cognition: A New Foundation for Design*. Ablex Publishing (Language and Being).

Wittgenstein, L. (2010) *Philosophical Investigations*. John Wiley & Sons.

Woessner, M. (2010) *Heidegger in America*. Cambridge University Press.

Cambridge Elements

The Philosophy of Martin Heidegger

About the Editors
Filippo Casati
Lehigh University

Filippo Casati is an Assistant Professor at Lehigh University. He has published an array of articles in such venues as *The British Journal for the History of Philosophy*, *Synthese*, *Logic et Analyse*, *Philosophia*, *Philosophy Compass* and *The European Journal of Philosophy*. He is the author of *Heidegger and the Contradiction of Being* (Routledge) and, with Daniel O. Dahlstrom, he edited *Heidegger on Logic* (Cambridge University Press).

Daniel O. Dahlstrom
Boston University

Daniel O. Dahlstrom, John R. Silber Professor of Philosophy at Boston University, has edited twenty volumes, translated Mendelssohn, Schiller, Hegel, Husserl, Heidegger, and Landmann-Kalischer, and authored Heidegger's *Concept of Truth* (2001), *The Heidegger Dictionary* (2013; second extensively expanded edition, 2023), *Identity, Authenticity, and Humility* (2017) and over 185 essays, principally on 18th–20th century German philosophy. With Filippo Casati, he edited *Heidegger on Logic* (Cambridge University Press).

About the Series
A continual source of inspiration and controversy, the work of Martin Heidegger challenges thinkers across traditions and has opened up previously unexplored dimensions of Western thinking. The Elements in this series critically examine the continuing impact and promise of a thinker who transformed early twentieth-century phenomenology, spawned existentialism, gave new life to hermeneutics, celebrated the truthfulness of art and poetry, uncovered the hidden meaning of language and being, warned of "forgetting" being, and exposed the ominously deep roots of the essence of modern technology in Western metaphysics. Concise and structured overviews of Heidegger's philosophy offer original and clarifying approaches to the major themes of Heidegger's work, with fresh and provocative perspectives on its significance for contemporary thinking and existence.

Cambridge Elements

The Philosophy of Martin Heidegger

Elements in the Series

Heidegger on Being Affected
Katherine Withy

Heidegger on Eastern/Asian Thought
Lin Ma

Heidegger on Poetic Thinking
Charles Bambach

Heidegger's Concept of Science
Paul Goldberg

Heidegger on Religion
Benjamin D. Crowe

Heidegger on Thinking
Lee Braver

A full series listing is available at: www.cambridge.org/EPMH

For EU product safety concerns, contact us at Calle de José Abascal, 56–1°, 28003 Madrid, Spain or eugpsr@cambridge.org.